Green Monasticism

The Gethsemani Encounters

The first Gethsemani Encounter was held in 1996 and came about in response to a request made by His Holiness the Dalai Lama. He had taken part in a Buddhist/Catholic dialogue on "*Kenosis* and Emptiness" at the Parliament for the World's Religions in Chicago in 1993. At its conclusion he suggested that there be a sequel in a monastic setting, where he could be "a monk among monks." He expressed his hope that such a gathering could take place at Gethsemani Abbey, the monastery of Thomas Merton, whom he had met in India in 1968, a little more than a month before Merton's accidental death in Bangkok on December 10.

The theme of the first Gethsemani Encounter was the spiritual life in the Buddhist and Christian monastic traditions. The meeting brought together an international group of about fifty leading Buddhist and Catholic practitioners and teachers of spirituality, both monastic and lay. The second Gethsemani Encounter took place in 2002, in which North American Buddhist and Christian practitioners who had been in dialogue with each other since the first Gethsemani Encounter addressed the subject of suffering and its transformation from their respective traditions. The third Gethsemani Encounter, which occurred in 2008, involved a discussion on Buddhist and Christian responses to the environmental crisis.

Gethsemani I
The Spiritual Life
A Dialogue of Buddhist and Christian Monastics
Edited by James A. Wiseman and Donald W. Mitchell

Gethsemani II
Finding Peace in Troubled Times
Buddhist and Christian Monastics on Transforming Suffering
Edited by James A. Wiseman and Donald W. Mitchell

Gethsemani III
Green Monasticism
A Buddhist–Catholic Response to an Environmental Calamity
Edited by Donald W. Mitchell and William Skudlarek, OSB

Green Monasticism

A Buddhist–Catholic Response to an Environmental Calamity

Edited by
Donald W. Mitchell
and
William Skudlarek, OSB

Lantern Books ♦ New York
A Division of Booklight Inc.

2010
Lantern Books
128 Second Place
Brooklyn, NY 11231
www.lanternbooks.com

Copyright © 2010 Monastic Interreligious Dialogue

Printed in the United States of America

Library of Congress Cataloging-in-Publication Data

Green monasticism : a Buddhist-Catholic response to an environmental calamity / edited by Donald Mitchell and William Skudlarek.
   p. cm.
  ISBN-13: 978-1-59056-167-6 (alk. paper)
  ISBN-10: 1-59056-114-7
  1. Monastic and religious life—Congresses. 2. Human ecology—Religious aspects—Catholic Church—Congresses. 3. Monastic and religious life (Buddhism)—Congresses. 4. Human ecology—Religious aspects—Buddhism—Congresses. 5. Catholic Church—Relations—Buddhism—Congresses. 6. Buddhism—Relations—Catholic Church—Congresses. I. Mitchell, Donald. II. Skudlarek, William.
  BX2440.G74 2010
  201'.7708820657—dc22

                          2009040334

Simple and Sufficient

Statement of Understanding and Commitment

Gethsemani III

Spread with garlands of vines,
Places delighting the mind,
Resounding with elephants,
Appealing:
Those rocky crags
Refresh me.
— *Theragatha 18:*
Mahakassapa

The wolf and the lamb shall
    graze alike
And the lion shall eat hay like
    the ox.
None shall hurt or destroy
On all my holy mountain, says
    the Lord
—*Isaiah 65:25*

We live in a time of environmental crisis and calamity, but also in a time when more and more people are coming together to respond to the suffering of the world. Our monastic interreligious dialogue has brought us to a new awareness of the social and spiritual relevance of ancient monastic traditions that have been sustained for millennia by Buddhist and Catholic communities.

Together we celebrate our common monastic values of reverence for the sacredness of all things, contemplation, humility, simplicity, compassion, and generosity. These virtues contribute to a life of nonviolence, balance, and contentment with sufficiency.

We recognize greed and apathy as the poisons at the heart of ecological damage and unbridled materialism. Throughout the centuries, monastic life has inspired generous personal, social, and spiritual effort for the good of others. We give and receive in the spirit of gratitude.

We acknowledge our complicity in damaging the environment and will make a sincere and sustained effort to reduce our negative impact on the planet. We are committed to take more mindful, universal responsibility for the way we use and manage the earth's resources. We resolve to develop our hearts and minds in ways that will contribute to a sustainable and hopeful future for our planet. We renew our commitment to the sacredness of the earth, relating to it as a community, not a commodity.

May our love for all beings and this world sustain our efforts and may our earth be revitalized. This is our prayer and commitment.

Contents

IV
Monasticism and the Consumer Society

V
Contemporary Environmental Practices
in American Monastic Communities

Bad Practices Hidden or Justified by Ideology

Good Practices, Ancient and Emerging

VI
Epilogue: Insights from Dialogue
Challenges to Living a Green Spirituality

VII
Appendix

Acknowledgments

Monastic Interreligious Dialogue expresses its gratitude to the monks of Gethsemani Abbey, who provided room, board, meeting facilities, and transportation for this encounter. It also thanks the institutions and individuals whose major grants and sustaining contributions made it possible to convoke a Buddhist/Christian dialogue on Monasticism and the Environment and to disseminate its proceedings.

Special grants
  The Raskob Foundation
  The Council of Presidents of American Benedictine Federations
      and Congregations
  Saint Procopius Abbey
  Mrs. Shirley Lotz

Sustaining contributions from Benedictine, Trappist, and Trappistine monastic communities in Canada and the United States

Women's communities in

1.	Atchison, Kans.	8.	Cottonwood, Idaho	15.	Fort Smith, Ark.
2.	Beech Grove, Ind.	9.	Crookston, Minn.	16.	Glendora, Calif.
3.	Bismarck, N.D.	10.	Dubuque, Iowa	17.	Jonesboro, Ark.
4.	Boerne, Tex.	11.	Duluth, Minn.	18.	Lisle, Ill.
5.	Bristow, Va.	12.	Eau Claire, Wis.	19.	Madison, Wis.
6.	Canyon, Tex.	13.	Erie, Pa.	20.	Nanaimo, B.C.
7.	Clyde, Mo.	14.	Ferdinand, Ind.	21.	Ogden, Utah

22. Redwoods, Calif.
23. Richardton, N.D.
24. Rock Island, Ill.
25. Saint-Benoît-Labre, Quebec
26. Saint Joseph, Minn.
27. Saint Leo, Fla.
28. Saint Marys, Pa.
29. Saint Paul, Minn.
30. Sainte-Marthe-Sur-Lac, Quebec
31. Virginia Dale, Colo.
32. Warren, Ohio
33. Watertown, S.D.
34. Winnipeg, Manitoba
35. Yankton, S.D.

Men's communities in

1. Atchison, Kans.
2. Aurora, Ill.
3. Belmont, N.C.
4. Benet Lake, Wis.
5. Big Sur, Calif.
6. Chicago, Ill.
7. Collegeville, Minn.
8. Conception, Mo.
9. Elmira, N.Y.
10. Huntsville, Utah
11. Jerome, Idaho
12. Lacey, Wash.
13. Latrobe, Pa.
14. Lisle, Ill.
15. Marvin, S.D.
16. Mepkin, S.C.
17. Mistassini, Quebec
18. Morristown, N.J.
19. Mount Angel, Ore.
20. Muenster, Sask.
21. Peosta, Iowa
22. Peru, Ill.
23. Portsmouth, R.I.
24. Richardton, N.D.
25. Rogersville, N.B.
26. Saint-Benoît-du-Lac, Quebec
27. Saint David, Ariz.
28. Saint Meinrad, Idaho
29. Schuyler, Neb.
30. Spencer, Mass.
31. Subiaco, Ark.
32. Vina, Calif.
33. Washington, D.C.
34. Weston, Vt.

Introduction

Why should monks, men and women, think they have something to say about caring for the environment? After all, haven't they opted to flee the world?

In the West, at least, that common misunderstanding of monastic life comes from a mistaken interpretation of *"fuga mundi,"* a Latin expression frequently found in medieval monastic literature. Literally translated, those words do, in fact, mean "flight of [i.e., from] the world." However, the word "world" in this context refers not to our natural surroundings, not even to human society absolutely speaking, but to all that is opposed to goodness and truth.

The history of monasticism—a particular way of living in the world that originated in India some three thousand years ago and then appeared in the Western world about a thousand years later—actually reveals that monks have generally appreciated, even celebrated, their natural environment and have been careful to avoid any action that would damage or disfigure it. Jain and Hindu insistence on not harming (*ahimsa*), Buddhist teaching on nonattachment (*upadana*), and Western monasticism's emphasis on being rooted in one place (*stabilitas loci*), have ensured, each in its own way, that monks treat the natural world with reverence and walk lightly through it. A rich tradition of preserving and beautifying their natural surroundings leads monks to believe their way of life can offer guidance and encouragement to a society that is finally coming to grips with the realization that it will have to treat the world differently if there is to be a world to

I

pass on to future generations. The "Statement of Understanding and Commitment" at the beginning of this book is one expression of their desire to share their values and traditions with all who search for ways to live in harmony with the world they are a part of.

The essays that make up Green Monasticism are, for the most part, edited versions of talks given at a Buddhist/Catholic encounter entitled "Monasticism and the Environment," held at Gethsemani Abbey in Kentucky, May 27–31, 2008. The conference was the third "Gethsemani Encounter" sponsored by Monastic Interreligious Dialogue (MID), an organization of North American Benedictines and Cistercians dedicated to fostering dialogue between Catholic monastics and spiritual practitioners of various religious traditions.[1]

(This was by no means the first attempt to bring religious practitioners and scholars together to explore their faith traditions and the environment. Most notably, perhaps, between 1996 and 1998, the Forum on Religion and Ecology (FORE) organized a series of conferences on religion and ecology at Harvard's Center for the Study of World Religions, from which ten books were produced, including Buddhism and Ecology and Christianity and Ecology. More on FORE's work can be found at http://fore.research.yale.edu.)

The first Gethsemani Encounter was held in 1996 and came about in response to a request made by His Holiness the Dalai Lama. He had taken part in a Buddhist/Catholic dialogue entitled "Kenosis and Emptiness" at the Parliament for the World's Religions in Chicago in 1993. At its conclusion he suggested that there be a sequel in a monastic setting, where he could be "a monk among monks." He expressed his hope that such a gathering could take place at Gethsemani Abbey, the monastery of Thomas Merton, whom he had met in India in 1968, a little more than a month before Merton's accidental death in Bangkok on December 10.

The theme of the first Gethsemani Encounter was the spiritual life in the Buddhist and Christian monastic traditions. The meeting brought together an international group of about fifty leading Buddhist and Catholic practitioners and teachers of spirituality, both monastic and lay. The proceedings were published in *The Gethsemani Encounter: A Dialogue on the Spiritual Life by Buddhist and Christian Monastics.*[2]

The second Gethsemani Encounter took place in 2002. At this gathering North American Buddhist and Christian practitioners who had been in dialogue with one another since the first Gethsemani Encounter addressed the subject of suffering and its transformation from their respective traditions. The proceedings were published under the title *Transforming Suffering: Reflections on Finding Peace in Troubled Times.*[3]

As MID began planning a Buddhist/Christian dialogue on monasticism and the environment, it was obvious that Gethsemani would be the ideal place to meet. Not only had two major interreligious encounters already taken place in that setting, but Thomas Merton, the abbey's most well-known monk, had been a pioneer in raising awareness about threats to our environment. He also was one of the first spiritual writers to call attention to the importance—indeed, the necessity—of interreligious dialogue, especially for monks, in addressing the world's problems.

The opening presentation at Gethsemani III was therefore devoted to Merton's analysis of the ecological catastrophe brought about by rapid industrialization and a growing inability to see nature as anything more than a resource to be exploited for economic advantage. In "Paradise Regained Re-lost" Father Ezekiel Lotz of Mount Angel Abbey in Oregon argues that Merton's attraction to monastic life, and in particular to the Trappist form of monastic life, which in the 1940s was still founded on a self-sustaining agricultural model, sprang from his longing to regain paradise. Within a few years of his entrance into the monastic community at Gethsemani, however, a centuries' old way of life changed almost overnight as the monastery modernized its farming methods and started marketing cheeses and fruitcakes in order to increase income and avert impending bankruptcy.

Merton was very critical of the rapid and—to his mind—uncritical way in which this transformation took place. The loss of the bucolic life he had hoped to find in the monastery, coupled with his growing awareness of the imminence of a global ecological catastrophe, brought him to the edge of despair. In one of his last working notebooks, Lotz found this marginal note: "The dreadful fact [is] that I was born into this world at the very moment when the whole thing came to a head; it is precisely in my lifetime that civilization has undergone this massive attack from within itself. My whole life is shaped by this. . . . It presses on the brain with a (near) darkness."[4]

Merton's fear that the forces of destruction were too far advanced to be reversed only seemed to heighten his appreciation for the beauty of the world around him. His journal and other writings are filled with evocative descriptions of plants and animals, times and seasons. Just a few years before Gethsemani III a beautiful anthology of his writings on nature had appeared, making it possible to begin each session of the encounter with the reading of an appropriate text from Merton, followed by a time for reflection.[5]

Buddhist practitioner Stephanie Kaza, a professor in the environmental program at the University of Vermont and a scholar of Buddhist environmental thought, opened the first full day of the encounter with a PowerPoint presentation on the magnitude, scope, and seriousness of the ecological catastrophe at our doorstep. Her presentation provided observable and scientifically verifiable evidence that the global environmental crisis is extremely grave and multifaceted, involving species and habitat loss; increasingly unsustainable human populations; the diminishment of food, water, and basic, nonrenewable resources; the broadening and depleting environmental impact of new technologies; the rapid rise of consumerist economies in China, India, and Southeast Asia; threats to an oil-based global economy; and the widespread impacts of climate change.

One of the major reasons for this multifaceted crisis is that 74 percent of the earth's biocapacity is consumed by only five countries or regions of the world: India, China, Europe, Japan, and the United States. Using the metaphor of an "ecological footprint" to refer to the load imposed by a given population on nature (more specifically, to refer to the land area necessary to sustain current levels of consumption and waste discharge), Kaza then compared the footprints left by these five regions. As is clearly evident from the following figures, the United States, with only 4.5 percent of the world's population, uses and consumes a vastly disproportionate amount of the world's resources:

	Percentage of the world's population	Ecological footprint (acres) per person	Percentage of global biocapacity
India	17.1	1.9	7
China	19.4	3.9	18
Europe	10.8	11.6	19
Japan	1.8	11.8	5
United States	4.5	23.9	25

The reason for this extraordinarily high level of consumption in the United States is the epidemic of "affluenza," an insatiable desire to use and possess more and more things. A few random indicators from 2002 show just how serious this disease is: "Our annual production of solid waste would fill a convoy of garbage trucks stretching halfway to the moon. We have twice as many shopping centers as high schools. ... A CEO now earns 475 times as much as the average worker, a tenfold increase since 1980. Since 1950, we Americans have used up more resources than everyone who ever lived on earth before them."[6]

Kaza concluded her presentation by emphasizing the important role that faith-based organizations can play in responding to the ever-increasing damage being done to the environment. What these religious bodies especially need to do is to raise consciousness and show, in word and deed, that care for the environment is an ethical and spiritual imperative. Their message will be all the more convincing if different religious groups can work together on environmental projects—land restoration or community gardens, for example—or share such physical resources as retreat centers or meeting areas.

Two presentations on the different philosophical/theological contexts in which Buddhist and Christian monasticism are rooted precede essays on monastic teachings on nature and monastic practices that guide our relationship with it. Ajahn Punnadhammo, a Theravadin monk of the Thai Forest tradition who lives at the Arrow River Forest Hermitage in Ontario, draws on the Buddhist teaching of dependent origination to address the causes and conditions behind the current climate crisis. He points out that dependent origination, not a deity, is the ultimate cause of the objects and events of the universe. Keeping in mind that the twelve stages of dependent origination are to be seen as a dynamic ongoing process, not as a linear movement through historical time, he traces the cause of climate change back to the desire for pleasures of the senses. Sensory desire gives rise to consumerism, consumerism gives rise to commodity production, commodity production gives rise to resource extraction, resource extraction gives rise to greenhouse gas release, and greenhouse gas release gives rise to climate change. He proposes that the reason so many contemporary attempts to solve the crisis—by switching to biofuels, for example—are ineffective, or even counterproductive, is that they do not address the root cause of the problem. It is precisely because the monastic virtues of nongreed, contentment, and reconnecting to the interdependent web of life do address the root cause of our ecological crisis that monasticism can make a valuable contribution to the contemporary green movement.

In his presentation on the Catholic doctrine of creation, James Wiseman of Saint Anselm's Abbey in Washington, DC, recognizes that a literal interpretation of anthropomorphic descriptions of God creating matter *ex nihilo* or fashioning human beings out of clay will elicit unbelief and even ridicule. The doctrine of creation attempts to respond to the "why" question of material and sentient existence, rather than to the "how" question of the origin of the universe. There continue to be disputed questions in the Christian theology of creation. What is not disputed is that the material world is good, and that the only reason the universe continues to exist is because it is totally dependent on God's ongoing creative love. This love, Wiseman suggests, generates a "fellowship of creation" with an interdependence of which we are a part. This calls for both loving care and selfless nonattachment for the good of the cosmos as basic to solving our ecological problems today.

These two presentations make clear that while Buddhists and Christians do indeed differ in the way they regard the origin of the world, both believe that mind (Christians might say "spirit") is primary.[7] The principal difference would seem to lie in the Christian doctrine of a personal God. Both Buddhism and Christianity have a sense of the transcendental, but Buddhism is very reluctant to give the transcendental the attributes of a person or the characteristics of a first cause. The difference in our understanding of the material world is at a high level, and quite narrow and subtle. But as Punnadhammo and Wiseman show, and subsequent essays will confirm, the difference in understanding is hardly—if at all—reflected in the practices by which monks over the centuries have expressed their care for the world.

The subsequent two essays explain how the world and our life in it are treated by monastic rules. Rev. Heng Sure discusses the Patimokkha/Pratimoksha (in the Theravada traditions) and the Ten Major and Forty-eight Subsidiary *Bodhisattva* Precepts (in the Mahayana traditions). Sr. Judith Sutera discusses the Rule of Benedict. Heng Sure, a Chan monk from the Berkeley Buddhist Center, admits that Buddhist monastic rules, like their Christian equivalents, contain relatively few specifically environmental references as we would define them today. The reason we can look to the rules for wise guidance on how to live skillfully on the planet is that they are grounded in the principles of no greed, no harm, and interdependence. They reflect, he says, "the wisdom of earth-based peoples who have always known that nature is one texture, one fabric, and humanity is knit into it inextricably."

Sr. Judith Sutera of Mount Saint Benedict in Atchison, Kansas, also notes that Saint Benedict never mentions a specific love for nature or a concern for ecology, nor does he acknowledge the relationship between the monastic community and nature. Certain sections of his Rule, however, read like a description of the way people relate to the world around them when they believe that the kingdom of God is here and now. To demonstrate her point she contextualizes and expands on a couple of brief passages in the Rule: that all things "are to be treated as vessels of the altar" (chapter 31), and that "whoever fails to keep the things belonging to the monastery clean or treats them carelessly should be reproved" (chapter 32). Being mindful that all material things have been given as gifts, using them properly, and then giving them back undamaged is the way people act when they believe the good news that the kingdom of God is not to be found in some far-off utopia, but is coming into being in our midst.

What then are the principal characteristics of the monastic way of relating to the environment? They can best be summed up as reverence, renunciation, gratitude, and generosity. Abbot Eko Little of Shasta Abbey in Mount Shasta, California, draws on the deep and far-reaching religious vision of Eihei Dogen (1200–1252 CE), the founder of the Soto Zen tradition in Japan, presenting him as a luminary of the monastic view of the environment as well as a prophet of a sacred and sustainable environmental culture. For Dogen it was not enough to say that all beings are endowed with Buddha Nature or have Buddha Nature: everyone *is* Buddha Nature. And not just every *one*; every *thing* is Buddha Nature. The only way, then, to practice the Buddha Nature of every thing and every one is to venerate, revere, cherish, and take care of the world and everything in it. Echoing Sutera's comments about Benedict's rules for the cellarer to treat all things as sacred "vessels of the altar," Abbot Little shows how Dogen's rules for the Chief

Cook contain guidance for this type of religious care even for a "cooking pot or grain of rice."

For Fr. Charles Cummings from the Holy Trinity Trappist Monastery in Utah, simplicity is the key feature of the monastic way of life, a virtue that many contemporary monks find easier to hold as a spiritual ideal than to put into practice in their daily lives. Materially, simplicity is a life uncluttered by the superfluous and content with the necessary. Spiritually, simplicity is being centered on the one thing necessary, which Christians would identify as the love of God. A concern for simplicity has led monks to reject the superfluous and to discover that less, rather than more, is often more pleasing. But simplicity is a matter of justice, not just aesthetics. Many people—not only monks—choose to live simply so that others may simply live.

The formal presentations at Gethsemani III concluded with four talks on the actual environmental practices of Buddhist and Catholic monasteries in North America today. They begin with an examination of conscience (to use a Catholic expression) on unskillful practices (to use a Buddhist expression), either hidden or justified by ideology. They then conclude on a more positive note with two reports on some of the best practices to be found in North American monastic communities.

Unskillful practices in Buddhist communities, both monastic and lay, that negatively impact the environment are often the result of widespread misinterpretations of Buddhist teaching on equanimity, the relinquishing of desire, karma, and contentment that lead to apathy, indifference, and complacency. Another cause is the failure to recognize the meaning and importance of the Buddha's teaching on right and wise effort, which Ayya Tathaaloka Bhikkhuni of the Aranya Bodhi Awakening Forest Hermitage in Northern California describes as "the most widely unknown and most prevalently misunderstood of all of the basic Buddhist teachings . . . at least in America today, both in the public at large, as well as within the Buddhist community." She shows how this is the case in certain situations, but also shows how skillful application of correctly understood teachings of the Buddha can give a strong witness today as to how to address the contemporary environmental crises.

Within Catholic monasticism, as Fr. Hugh Feiss of Ascension Monastery in Jerome, Idaho, points out, bad theological arguments are sometimes used to justify bad practices. One example is the rationalization that since God gave us humans dominion over the earth, we are free to do what we want. The main justifications, however, tend to be cultural or psychological. Like the society they are still a part of, monks fall victim to the seduction of marketing and advertising, mistake good intentions for action, and make decisions based on what is most "practical." As do many of their contemporaries, they too can respond to notices of impending ecological disaster with the psychological mechanisms of denial, repression, or projection. In order to turn toward the earth with reverence and care, confident that they will find its Ground and Goal, monks need to confess and lament their complicity in the illusions that have brought the world to the current crisis.

Ven. Thubten Semkye of Sravasti Abbey in Newport, Washington, and Sr. Renée Branigan of Sacred Heart Monastery in Richardton, North Dakota, offer specific examples of environmentally sound practices in North American Buddhist and Catholic monasteries, practices that reflect fundamental monastic values coupled with an awareness of the seriousness of the contemporary environmental crisis. Buddhist monastic communities are relatively new in North America and often follow environmentally friendly practices for using resources and for care of the land. The monasteries provide guidance by teaching and example for lay Buddhist practitioners. Catholic monastic communities, on the other hand, began forming in the mid-nineteenth century. Most of them had early days of poverty ranging from dire to not so bad, and then, from the early to the mid-twentieth century, experienced a period of explosive growth, both in numbers and in material resources. Looking back over the past 150 years of Catholic monastic life in North America, Sr. Renée observes that most Catholic monastic communities started out environmentally friendly by necessity, strayed as they became more established and comfortable, and now are trying to act responsibly out of a tight blend of fiscal necessity and good ecological intentions. But they are finding that making ecologically sound decisions and then implementing them is more costly and more complicated than they had imagined.

Following the presentations that were given at Gethsemani III, there are two essays, one by a Buddhist, the other by a Catholic participant in the encounter, that address some of the challenges of living a green spirituality. In his essay, Ajahn Sona from the Buddhist community at Birken Forest Monastery points out that Buddhism creates a helpful context for environmentalism by providing practices to rid oneself of the self-polluting emotions that sometimes fuel well-meaning environmentalists. Fueled by his healthy, positive, and natural attitude, his community has made a number of decisions concerning its mode of living that have made it a model for a green monasticism of simplicity and sufficiency. Sr. Anne McCarthy of the Benedictine Sisters of Erie reflects on how the prophetic dimension of monasticism can be, and indeed must be, expressed by action that responds to both the cry of nature and the cry of the poor. The devastation of our environment hurts us all, but it is those who are already impoverished who suffer the most. By linking their concern for the protection of the environment to compassionate action that alleviates the suffering and recognizes the dignity of the poor of the world—especially those in their own backyards—monastic men and women give powerful witness that, ultimately, it is love that changes everything.

Following the epilogue is an appendix with the English translation of an article by Fabrice Blée entitled "La spiritualité chrétienne du dialogue, creuset d'une nouvelle conscience écologique," literally, "The Christian Spirituality of Dialogue, Crucible of a new Ecological Consciousness." It was originally published in the April 2008 issue of *La Chair et le Souffle*. The author, a Regular Professor on the Faculty of Theology of the University of Saint Paul, Ottawa, where he teaches in the areas of the interreligious dialogue and Christian spirituality, wrote his doctoral dissertation on the history of the North American Commission of Monastic Interreligious Dialogue. Drawing on Buddhist and Christian sources in his essay, he makes the case that a Christian spirituality of dialogue favors the adoption of a new way of thinking about nature and of entering into a faith-inspired relationship with it. It provides a fitting conclusion to this collection of essays by Buddhist and Christian monks who hope the way of life they have received from their forebears may offer guidance and inspiration to all who are dedicated to saving a world that is teetering on the brink of disaster.

Guidance and inspiration are the key words here. Gethsemani III was an encounter on monastic practice and monastic spirituality *in relation to* the current ecological crisis. Rather than intentionally setting out to come up with specific proposals to solve the crisis caused by global warming, the destruction of species, and the poisoning of our land and water, the Buddhist and Christian monks who came together at the home of Thomas Merton wanted to arrive at a deeper understanding of the connections between the way of life to which they had committed themselves and the environment in which they live it out. They came to Gethsemani believing that monastic teachings and traditions continue to offer a valuable guide for living at peace with one another and with all beings. Their hope is that by dedicating themselves to their monastic calling with renewed generosity and greater focus on the environmental crisis, they will model a way of life that will be attractive and compelling to those who are not monks in the formal sense of the word, and that the world will be a healthier place for it.

—William Skudlarek, OSB

I

Thomas Merton and the Looming
Ecological Crisis

Paradise Regained Re-lost

Fr. Ezekiel Lotz, OSB

In two letters written between the years 1964 and 1965, one to a newspaper correspondent and the other to an Anglican woman, the Trappist monk and author Fr. Mary Louis Merton, better known to his reading public as Thomas Merton, ruminated about what and how he would have changed in his by-then classic autobiographical "confessions," *The Seven Storey Mountain*, published some sixteen years before. Merton contended that he would have "said many things differently" and that his "thought at the time was hardly mature." Shortly before he died in 1968, Merton, writing to a high school student in California, noted that if he were to rewrite his most popular book, and the work that had put him on the map as a spiritual voice to be reckoned with, he would "cut out a lot of the sermons . . . and sales pitch for Catholic schools and that."[1]

And yet, as Merton scholar and past president of the International Thomas Merton Society William H. Shannon points out in his literary-critical biography of Merton entitled *Something of a Rebel*, *The Seven Storey Mountain* continues to attract, and play a major role in the conversion processes and vocational discernment experiences of, men and women around the planet. Vivid and specific narrative accounts of his childhood and young adulthood, the personal sincerity and genuineness of the author, as well as the perennial human elements included in the book give Merton's masterpiece its ongoing appeal. As early as 1951, *The Seven Storey Mountain* had gone into its 254th printing.[2]

Monsignor Shannon's eight-page reader's guide to *The Seven Storey Mountain* included in *Something of a Rebel* provides the first-time reader with a good overview and some helpful hints about hidden, lost, as well as some of the more obvious and traditional themes that support and serve as framework for this postmodern "confessions." But one major theme that Shannon fails to note and that many Merton critics seemed to neglect or to ignore up until about a decade or so ago, even though it is a seminal component throughout the rest of his writings (journals and letters included) right up until the time of his death, is Merton's ongoing concern with what historian Peter Laslett has referred to as "the world we have lost." That is to say, a world operating on a natural and balanced level, untrammeled and not held captive by a technology and science that seem to have all but surpassed the control of its creators and finally and very frighteningly run amok.[3]

The young Thomas Merton's childhood experiences growing up on a still predominantly rural Long Island in New York, his sojourns among French peasants while a boy accompanying his artist-father on his painting expeditions through Europe, his confrontation with an increasingly frenetic, technologically advanced, albeit emotionally and spiritually bankrupt society while a young man at Cambridge and Columbia universities, all culminate in his decision to enter what was still at the time a medievally structured Trappist abbey in rural Kentucky. Merton became a monk at the peak of the Second World War, a time when a good part of the planet felt that the entire world was coming apart at the seams.

The paradisiacal world of a garden wilderness that was being subsumed and demolished by increasingly meaningless modes of materialism, genocidal nationalist bigotry, and means of warfare, the power of which humanity had only had nightmares about in the past, was regained by the new novice Mary Louis Merton upon his entry into the rigorously cloistered and liturgically rich life of Our Lady of Gethsemani Abbey. Merton's friends and associates who attended his solemn vows and ordination to the priesthood some five years after his entry noted during their celebratory conversations afterward that the previously boisterous, unfocused rake who had been Tom Merton had blossomed and come into his own while living in a community where the inhabitants still grew their own food, made their own shoes, and arose in the middle of the night to chant psalms and sing hymns for sometimes as long as three hours at a shot.

Before long, however, there was to be trouble in paradise, a not uncommon occurrence in supposedly paradisiacal settings in both modern and postmodern societies. We will discuss Merton's understanding of, and reaction to, that issue in more detail. First, however, we should consider two important passages from *The Seven Storey Mountain* that both foreshadow and summarize the themes of technology and its effects on the world and its varied inhabitants in the modern and postmodern age. Reviewing these incidents in the young Merton's life will also supply us with an example of a forceful juxtaposition of experiences that powerfully affected and influenced the boy and then the young man who was Tom Merton.

The first experience is that of a twelve-year-old spending the Christmas holiday of 1926 visiting his father in the village of Murat, located in the old Celtic province of the Auvergne.

As Merton describes it in *The Seven Storey Mountain,* this is a mountainous region of central France, whose valleys are richly pastured and whose mountains are "heavy with fir trees" or "covered in grass."[4] The Auvergnats are traditionally scoffed at by the other French for their "simplicity and rusticity" but are, at least in Merton's estimation, very stolid but very good people. The village where the young Tom spent this holiday break was covered in snow that set off the gray and blue "slate-dark pattern" of buildings grouped along three hillsides. His hosts, M. and Mme. Privat, were a typical Auvergnat couple, both no more than five feet tall: he, broad shouldered, a solid column of

muscle and bone; she, "thin, serious, earnest, and quick," with a traditional sugar-loaf headdress perched on her head in seeming complement to her husband's black, broad-brimmed hat. What impressed
itself upon the young Merton, and all of what stays with him over the
next fifteen years until he enters Gethsemani and comes to write his
early memoirs, is this: ". . . I no longer possess any details about them.
I just remember their kindness and goodness to me, and their peace-
fulness and utter simplicity. They inspired real reverence, and I think,
in a way, they were certainly saints. And they were saints in that most
effective and telling way: sanctified by leading ordinary lives in a completely supernatural way, sanctified by obscurity, by usual skills, by
common tasks, by routine, but skills, tasks, routine which received a
supernatural form from grace within. . . ."[5] Merton would later return
to live with this couple and their family for a two-week period in the
summer, when they fed young Tom "plenty of butter and milk," but
also nourished him with a supernatural love full of a delicate solici-
tude, which the young monk-writer Merton is certain had an effect on
his future conversion and vocation.

The second incident comes some eight years after Merton's short
sojourn in the natural paradise of the Auvergne and finds him in what he
describes as the "dark, sinister" atmosphere of Cambridge University.

In fact, Cambridge is, in the metaphorical geography of *The Seven
Storey Mountain*, the lowest circle of hell. The institution and its people
are like some kind of animal that gores him so deeply "that he felt that
he would never recover entirely from the wound."[6] Merton certainly
had become a different person by the time he entered Clare College at
Cambridge in the autumn of 1933. Almost all of his friends at university seemed to be those who had made it onto the proctors' books for
"the hundred and one university crimes that came under the general
heading of 'conduct unbecoming of a gentleman.'"[7] When he comes to
write *The Seven Storey Mountain* and ruminate on what exactly was
wrong with Cambridge and the people who were there, why they were
so "empty" inside, Merton relates the following incident:

When I had been away from Cambridge for about a year, I heard what happened to . . . a friend of mine. . . . Mike was a beefy and red-faced and noisy youth . . . and was part of the crowd in which I milled around. . . . He was full of loud laughter and a lot of well-meaning exclamations, and in his quieter moments he got into long and complicated sentences about life. But what was most characteristic of him was that he liked to put his fist through windows. He was the noisy and hearty type; he was altogether jolly. A great eater and drinker, he chased after girls with an astonishing heaviness of passion and emotion. He managed to get into a lot of trouble. [After leaving Cambridge] . . . I heard how he ended up. The porter, or somebody, went down into the showers, under the buildings of the Old Court at Clare, and found Mike hanging by his neck from a rope slung over one of the pipes, with his big hearty face black with the agony of strangulation. He had hanged himself.[8]

All the important issues and images involving an ever-advancing technological society and its insidious effects on the natural world and those who populate it are in evidence here. And yet, even Merton himself, at least at this point, never really emphasizes them or gives them their due. Furthermore, as Merton's biographer Benjamin Mott has pointed out, Merton never objectively tells the reader of *The Seven Storey Mountain* just what that wound was that Cambridge and its inhabitants delivered to the young and ever-more-noticeably-out-of-control Tom Merton.

Not contained in *The Seven Story Mountain*, but referred to obliquely in various conversations and journal entries over the rest of his life, is an event from that one year at Cambridge, before he was thrown out of the school and opted to return to the United States and Columbia University, the so-called Party in the Middle of the Night—a drunken, out-of-control gathering in November of 1934—in which a mock crucifixion took place, a crucifixion that, due to the besotted state of the participants, became, or very nearly became, an actual one.[9] Merton's naturalization papers for the U.S. government contain references to a scar on the palm of his right hand, and his literary agent for twenty-five years, Naomi Burton Stone, commenting on the mark to Merton, noted that he referred to it rather uneasily as his "stigmata."[10] Various coded allusions (something for which he was famous throughout his writing career) about crucifixion crop up in Merton's writings at this time, both in prose and in poetry, most especially in connection to characters and events linked to Cambridge. Indeed, certain pages that are now missing (either censored by the church or by Merton himself—something else for which he was renowned throughout his writing career) from a draft of his early, unpublished novel, *The Labyrinth*, include just such a crucifixion scene—a scene that Naomi Burton Stone was unable to forget after having read it in the manuscript draft. Although nothing definitive can be proven about this incident, there is a "good deal of circumstantial evidence" that suggests that Merton had added genuine sacrilege to his list of other transgressions accumulated during his one and only year at Cambridge.

Around the same time as the so-called Party in the Middle of the Night, Merton's great-aunt Maude Pearce (his paternal grandmother's sister) died and was buried at Ealing, in west London. Merton had used his Uncle Ben and Aunt Maude's home as base for a period just before and then immediately after his own father's untimely death. It is significant that this favorite and influential relative died right in the middle of Merton's Cambridge experience, when "every nerve and fiber of" his "being . . . was laboring to enslave" him "in the bonds" of what he called his "own intolerable disgust."[11] Aunt Maude was an emblem for Merton of an England different from the one that he was experiencing at Cambridge. She was warm, sensible, no-nonsense, innocent of heart. She represented the other England—the England of the "world we have lost" or that was in the process of disappearing: the bucolic England of William Blake's "green and pleasant land."[12] Thus, when

Maude dies, Merton notes in *The Seven Storey Mountain*, that at the funeral, "They committed the thin body of my poor Victorian angel to the clay of Ealing, and buried my childhood with her."[13]

Merton's search for this lost Garden of Eden of his childhood, for that bucolic, green, and pleasant land of Blake's poetry, was at least partially achieved once he entered the cloistered grounds of Gethsemani Abbey. It is his life at Gethsemani that we will now trace in terms of the restoration of this garden, of the life lived therein, a life of the "world we have lost"; and we will observe it in terms of the themes for this book: technology, ecology, and the monastic/contemplative life. Indeed, in a very uncanny and frightening way, the loss of this world of closeness to nature, of living on equal terms with the creation, and a sense sometimes of powerlessness in trying to salvage it and retain it in the face of an ever more chaotic technological society that we ourselves have created, was repeated in the monastery confines within the first five years of Merton's monastic life.

We have already noted the almost medieval quality of life at Gethsemani when Merton entered in December of 1941. Horses and plows were still employed by the monks to work the soil and harvest the crops. The monks themselves lived in open dormitories with no central heating, and private spaces were created with thin partitioning. They slept fully clothed in their habits on straw mattresses. Their meals, which were completely based on fresh vegetables and grains, were perhaps meager, but all the food was homegrown and freshly prepared. Work, most of which was manual labor in the forests or fields that surrounded the monastery, was plentiful even if the food was not. Cloister was rigorously observed. Monks lived, died, and were buried there[14]—with no coffin or embalming, and no name or date on the simple cross at the head of the grave. This was indeed a very different environment from that of Cambridge University, with its drunken revels and perhaps not-so-mock crucifixion scenes taking place late on a November's night. Yet Gethsemani is where Merton found his home for the next twenty-seven years, and the importance of physical setting and place is something that cannot be exaggerated for Thomas Merton.[15] Indeed, as William Shannon points out concerning the young novice's reaction to monastic life, "Merton loved every bit of it. He embraced the monastic discipline with the same enthusiasm as he had earlier thrown himself into the disordered, aimless pseudo-freedom of his youth."[16]

According to the twelfth-century mystical theologian Hugh of St. Victor, the recovery of Eden, whose very nature was unchangeable, was the aim of all human activity.[17] The monastery of Gethsemani was to have been, quite literally, this unchanging garden, this walled paradise for Merton and for so many others who entered and were formed with him. Any sense of the classically monastic notion of a *contemptus mundi*, of turning one's back on the world and society because it only distracts from the sole goal of the monk, which is God alone, does not last for long once Merton is inside the cloister walls. His early journal entries at Gethsemani abound in descriptions of the natural life around him and how it caused him to rejoice in the larger geography of God's garden.[18] The young Br. Louis writes after standing in the cloister doorway watching the sunset one evening, "I looked at all this in great tranquility, with my soul and spirit quiet. For me landscape seems to be important for contemplation ... anyway, I have no scruples about loving it."[19]

However, this place, which appeared to be "so stable" in the "unstable world in 1941,"[20] was very quickly and disconcertingly about to undergo significant and, for many of its inhabitants, disturbing changes within the first decade of Merton's life there. Along with the changes effected by 1951, a second wave of transformation (with buildings disappearing or others being gutted and altered) has made it next to impossible today to trace Merton's steps around the monastery environs as recorded in *The Seven Storey Mountain* or in *The Sign of Jonas*.

Although monasticism as lived at Gethsemani in the 1940s was far from perfect, the monks there experienced a simple and good life with most of the confreres living to an age far beyond the national average.[21] It was truly a communal or communist ethic that was being lived out there in reality—from each according to his capacity, to each according to his needs. Thus, the transformations that characterized the 1950s, greatly disturbing this equilibrium of capacity and needs, created a "new restlessness" in Merton, which the Gethsemani of 1941 not only had assuaged the anxiety of but had served to transform the young monk into a new man who had blossomed and grown into an ever-more integrated and balanced human person. Merton, both at the time and later in retrospect, would refer to these years as an "Edenic" period in his own life and in that of the community at Gethsemani.[22]

The changes commenced with the election of both a new abbot general of the Trappist Order in France and a new abbot at Gethsemani. This latter figure, Dom James Fox, was a graduate of Harvard Business School, and something of a prodigy in his field of expertise. He inherited a monastery that had survived on the heritage of its Alsatian-French founders for almost a hundred years, with little or no changes being made in its internal spiritual or external material existence. The result was that by the early 1950s, the monastery buildings desperately needed repair (especially with over a hundred monks in residence to house and feed) and the monastery economy desperately needed immediate attention, with the community being some $20,000 in debt.[23] Dom James, it seemed clear to everyone in the community, including Merton, was the man to effect the changes necessary. But were the compromises to the monastic life as it had been lived at Gethsemani for almost a hundred years going to be worth it in the long run? Perhaps one could only answer that question with hindsight. For Merton and a few others within the community, however, the consequences, many of them perhaps of a tragic and even a catastrophic nature, were all too clearly evident from very soon after the initiation of Dom James's reform.

The monastery needed to work on a more efficient basis, thus it needed to commit itself to greater activity.[24] Perhaps most significant was Dom James's decision to disband the old, medieval means of living self-sufficiently and instituting an active embracing of modern mechanized methods of farming and processing foods for personal consumption and commercial sale.[25] The changes, in a paradoxical way, paid off (for the time being), with wave after wave of novices applying for entrance to the cloister—so many in fact, that there was no room in the dormitories for them to sleep, and so pup tents were set up in the cloister garden for occupation. Nevertheless, this sudden growth was indeed paradoxical since, once the men had arrived and got a sample of the radical changes that were occurring at the abbey and witnessed the rapidly deteriorating system of socio-pastoral structures and spiritual symbols that were disappearing while the economic life of the now-mechanized abbey boomed and bustled, these very same vocations proceeded to leave in a steady exodus over the course of the next ten years.[26] As Michael Mott notes, the monastery had become not only one of economic soundness but one of actual financial prosperity. Yet, "like most financial achievements, this had costs which did not show up on the balance sheets. Some of the results of the changes were both spiritually and physically damaging. The achievement was an astonishing one, so much so that it tended to blind others."[27]

Merton, disturbed by the level of noise in and around the cloister brought on by the new heavy machinery in use, and furthermore by the fact that his own growing fame as an author was bringing in the needed cash with which to purchase the new jeeps, tractors, bulldozers, and combines, and so on, "saw the cost" to the community and recognized that it was much more than that his own personal "pastoral idyll had been shattered."[28] Not only was Merton concerned by the shift over to big business that was characterized by the monastery's new food-processing corporation, Gethsemani Farms (which produced and marketed cheese, bread, bacon, and the breeding of Belgian mares), but he was equally disturbed by the new methods of farming employed on the monastery farm proper. Insecticides and chemicals used by the monks seemed to give the crops a "forced color."[29]

This bothered Merton, as did the increasing number of dead birds he found on the property while taking hikes through the woods. In response to these occurrences, he wrote to Rachel Carson in January 1962 and even managed to have her ecologically provoking work *Silent Spring* read in the monastic refectory. The book was withdrawn, however, when the cellarer took issue with some of the figures and statistics that Carson quoted in her text.[30]

Merton's letter to Carson, which he marked for inclusion as an appendix to his so-called Cold War Letters, succinctly summarizes the situation as Merton saw it and served as a springboard for the many other reflections on technology and ecology that would weave themselves in and out of his writings for the next six years. First of all, he notes that there is a strange and perplexing contradiction seemingly inherent in the interrelationships of technology and ecology. There is the same mental process involved (Merton notes to Carson that he had almost written "mental illness" instead of process) in the human person's irresponsible propensity to "scorn the smallest values," while daring to use "our titanic power in a way that threatens not only civilization but life itself." This vicious circle of suicidal actions is repeated in our very attempts to cure the illness: "It seems that our remedies are instinctively those which aggravate the sickness: *the remedies are expressions of the sickness itself.*"[31]

There is a type of death wish—a Thanatos Syndrome, as Walker Percy termed it in his final novel—built right in to humankind's most fundamental being. Merton compares it to the Christian concept of original sin but notes that no matter what one's "dogmatic convictions," humans almost universally possess a "tendency to destroy and negate" themselves just "when everything is at its best, and that it is just when things are paradisiacal" that" we use our technological powers in a horrifyingly destructive manner.[32] Thus, there is a hatred of life lurking right under the surface of our optimism about ourselves and about our affluent society. But the economics, culture, philosophy of affluence is itself so self-defeating, contains "so many built-in frustrations" of its own, that it "inevitably leads us to despair."[33] The "awful fruit of this despair" is even more "indiscriminate, irresponsible destructiveness" and "hatred of life" (including hatred directed toward the natural world) to the point that in order "to 'survive' we instinctively destroy that on which our survival depends."[34] Furthermore, this destructive activity not only savages the natural resources of the world around us, it also eradicates the religious, spiritual systems that have for thousands of years assisted humans in maintaining a healthy balance between themselves and the planet on which they live. In the words of Donald P. St. John, "The technological system that has shattered nature's system of checks and balances, and promised godlike powers to humans, has simultaneously eroded cultural systems which generate virtues and a perennial wisdom that attempted to guard humanity from its own excesses."[35]

The appeal to a sapiential way of knowing and behaving is of crucial importance here as Merton shifts his discussion to an intentionally theological one, familiar ground for the seasoned monk in his cloistered paradise. To religious thinkers and sages, Merton notes to Carson, the "world has always appeared as a transparent manifestation of the love of God, as a 'paradise' of His wisdom, manifested in all His creatures . . . and in the most wonderful interrelationship between them." Merton now proposes what, in terms of Christian theology at least, has been dubbed the "stewardship model" of the human/rest-of-created-being interrelationship. Humankind's vocation within the context of the cosmic creation is to be as an eye to the rest of the body.[36] There is a "delicate balance" to maintain here, however, and humans must understand their position as one of profound responsibility, using nature wisely, "ultimately relating himself and visible nature to the invisible . . . to the source and exemplar of all being and all life."[37] It should come as no surprise to us, however, that Merton was not naïve about humans' failure to take on this responsibility supported by both an ecological and a cosmic wisdom.[38] Indeed, "the modern reluctance to accept such a simple yet sublime vocation is an essential piece to the puzzle of our violent and destructive behaviour towards creation."[39] But humans have been blinded into thinking that they do see all the better because they have acquired so much techno-logical know-how and power over the elements, and the blindness has led to the loss of our sense of "wisdom and cosmic perspective."[40] The stewardship model of ecological harmony and protection, no mat-ter how well intentioned and theologically well grounded, does not always, perhaps even rarely, work in the cold reality of postmodern technological society. As environmentalist William Schlesinger has so aptly stated, "Dominion over the Earth in Genesis didn't mean to leave it pillaged and smoking."[41] Nevertheless, the seemingly innate desire of humans to torch the very thing that sustains them and with which they need to cooperate in order to live integrally always seems to supersede the wise and cosmic perspective.

Merton concludes his theological exposition by noting that "tech-nics and wisdom are not by any means opposed. On the contrary, the duty of our age, the 'vocation' of modern man is to unite them in a supreme humility which will result in a totally self-forgetful creativity and service." He then poses the ten-million-dollar rhetorical question: "Can we do this?" And speculates that "Certainly we are not going in the right direction."[42]

Three years after his letter to Carson, Merton ruminated at length in *Conjectures of a Guilty Bystander* about the profound dilemma modern man was facing regarding technological development in rela-tion to an ever more pronounced ecological and societal disintegra-tion.[43] This remains perhaps the most developed commentary on these themes supplied by Merton in one place. For Merton, technol-ogy is falsely seen by most of society to be the "highest development of man," auguring a "golden age of plenty and perfect freedom." The technological achievements of modern humans are indeed "astonish-ing" and "magnificent." On the other hand, viewed from the context of their "unbalance" with the other aspects of "human existence in the world," they are components of "disintegration." Too much power in the hands of men only leads to the abuse of that power at the expense of "wisdom, prudence, [and] temperance." What difference does technological advancement make if the men and women in the society that possesses them are still frustrated, bored, suicidal, and megalomaniacal? He concludes:

> It does us no good to make fanatic progress if we do not know how to live with it, if we cannot make good use of it, and if, in fact, our technology becomes nothing more than an expensive and complicated way of cultural disintegration. It is bad form to say such things, to recognize such possibilities. But they are possibilities, and they are not often intelligently taken into account. People get emotional about them from time to time, and then sweep them away into forgetfulness. The fact remains that we have created for ourselves a culture which is not yet livable for mankind as a whole.[44]

In fact, the existence of a humanity ever more dependent on an emancipated technology for its necessities and its pleasures is one of "moral infancy, in total dependence not on 'mother nature' (such a dependence would be partly tolerable and human) but on a pseudo-nature of technology. . . ."[45] The subsequent illusion that "mechanical progress means human improvement" is what ultimately alienates humans from their own being and their own reality.[46]

> It is precisely because we are convinced that mechanical progress means human improvement, that alienates us from our own being and our own reality. It is precisely because we are convinced that our life . . . is better if we have a better car . . . TV set . . . toothpaste . . . that we condemn and destroy our own reality and the reality of our natural resources. Technology was made for man, not man for technology. In losing touch with being with God, we have fallen into a senseless

idolatry of production and consumption for their own sakes. We have renounced the act of being and plunged ourself into *process* for its own sake. We no longer know how to live, and because we cannot accept life in its reality life ceases to be a joy and becomes an affliction. And we even go so far as to blame God for it.[47]

Merton contrasts this equation of "technology equals manipulation of the created world equals progress equals happiness" to what instead should be openness and respect for the created world as God has given it to us. This respect and openness must be grounded in a real intuition of the act of being coupled with gratefulness for and a contemplative perception of being. If this is not the case, Merton warns, then we can look forward to "further destruction and debasement of the world in the name of a false humanism which has no other fruit than to make man hate himself, hate life, and hate the world he lives in."[48]

The material included in *Conjectures of a Guilty Bystander*, however, is not Merton's final word on the topic of technology and ecology. That is to be found in an occasional piece written for *Center Magazine* in July 1968, five months before his untimely death in Bangkok. One would be hard pressed to call this Merton's "mature" thought on the themes discussed in this book, but it does demonstrate that Merton was far from finished with the matter and that some of his original propositions had changed and developed in the years since his letter to Rachel Carson. In what is ostensibly a review of Roderick Nash's book *Wilderness and the American Mind*, Merton delves more deeply than ever before into the questions of technological society and ecology and religion's—most especially a contemplative religion's—role in the uniting and balancing of these two elements.

Merton begins his essay by once again noting the strange, paradoxical nature of humanity's current situation in a highly advanced technological society of affluence and unsurpassed power and control over its surroundings. It is an ambivalent culture full of self-contradictions, especially in its treatment of the wild.[49] We "confess our firm attachment to values that inexorably demand the destruction of the last remnant of wildness," but when people suggest that this contradiction is itself an "indication of a sickness in ourselves," we dismiss them as fanatics.[50] This sickness, Merton boldly states, is "rooted in our biblical, Judeo-Christian tradition," which he immediately notes is neither truly biblical nor Jewish nor Christian. Nevertheless, there is a nominally Christian approach to the world that at a deep and perhaps unconscious level is dualist in its metaphysics and as a result is "profoundly destructive of nature and of 'God's good creation.'"[51] Developing from their original Puritan forefathers' repugnance for spontaneity and so in turn for nature and the wild, the contemporary "American capitalist culture" finds itself "rooted in a secularized Christian myth and mystique of struggle with nature."[52]

The ambivalence continues with a second mystique layered on top of the first, this one being the cult of America the Beautiful, "America which must be kept lovely. . . . So don't throw that beer can in the river, even though the water is polluted with all kinds of industrial waste. Business can mess up nature, but not you, Jack!"[53] Henry David Thoreau—one of Merton's favorite authors on the topics at hand—and the Transcendentalists offer a more realistic and truthful assessment of the situation, but even their work is quickly turned into cliché-ridden propaganda by the powers that be. Yet Merton does make particular note of Thoreau's belief that humans need wildness to balance out their more civilizing tendencies, lest their propensity to "subject everything . . . to rational and conscious control" should "warp, diminish, and barbarize" them.[54]

Ultimately, Merton holds up Aldo Leopold and his now-classic book *A Sand County Almanac* as perhaps the best example of how we should approach the current conundrums of technology and ecology. Calling it one of "the most important moral discoveries of our time," Merton cites Leopold's "ecological conscience" as being "centered in an awareness of man's true place as a dependent member of the biotic community."[55] Leopold's rule-of-thumb ecological principle is that: "A thing is right when it tends to preserve the integrity, stability, and beauty of the biotic community. It is wrong when it tends otherwise."[56] Merton claims that "in light of this principle, an examination of our social, economic, and political history in the last hundred years would be a moral nightmare, redeemed only by a few gestures of good will on the part of those who obscurely realize that there is a problem. . . . [Compared] to the magnitude of the problem, their efforts are at best pitiful."[57] What is more, the old monster of self-contradicting hypocrisy rears its head again in that those who continue to rape nature simultaneously honor the wilderness myth with the same gestures and "great earnestness" of an Aldo Leopold or Henry David Thoreau.

Merton then re-asks the same question he had placed before Rachel Carson in 1962: Can Leopold's "ecological conscience become effective in America today?" Globally the situation looks bleak, Merton allows, especially when one considers that an ecological conscience is tantamount to a "peace-making conscience."[58] But with the stark examples of crop poisoning, defoliation of forest trees, and the "incineration of villages and their inhabitants with napalm" ever before his eyes, Merton does not hold much cause for hope. Acting locally may be the best we can hope for, and, at least in terms of his essay, wearing a "little yellow and red button" that proclaims "Celebrate life!" and bearing witness to this exhortation is about the best we can do given the present circumstances.

These are not the most promising of parting words from Merton on this matter. Up until the composition of this essay, he had always seen the monastery and the witness of the contemplative and sapiential life lived therein as one of the most important and effective means of combating the technological onslaught.

> The goal of the contemplative is, on its lowest level, the recognition of this splendour of being and unity—a splendour in which he is one with all that is. . . . Science and technology

are ... admirable in many respects ... but they can never solve [humanity's] deepest problems ... without wisdom ... [they] can only precipitate him still further into the centrifugal flight that flings him ... into the darkness of outer space. ...[59]

Already, by the time of *Conjectures of a Guilty Bystander*, Merton had become deeply worried that monastic institutions were having their mission and effectiveness weakened by the adoption of "modern production technologies."[60] If the cloister was to be a continual fore-taste of paradise until Christ's second coming, then it is our duty to "continue the work of paradise, by tending the garden."[61] For, the gar-den, the wilderness, is essential for contemplation,[62] or in the words of P. F. O'Connell, ". . . the work of paradise is the protection of cre-ation."[63] As Merton was to conclude in his long essay "Wilderness and Paradise," written in 1967:

> If the monk is a man whose whole life is built around a deeply religious appreciation of his call to wilderness and paradise ... and if technological society is constantly encroaching upon and destroying the remaining "wildernesses" which it never-theless needs in order to remain human, then we might sug-gest that the monk, of all people, should be ... anxious to preserve the wilderness in order to share it with those who need to come out from the cities and remember what it is like to be under trees and to climb mountains.[64]

Finally, Merton expressed in no uncertain terms this continuing concern with monasticism's ability to confront the conundrums of postmodern society during an informal talk delivered in Calcutta a few weeks before his untimely death in Bangkok:

> In the West there is now going on a great upheaval in monas-ticism, and much that is of undying value is being thrown

away irresponsibly, foolishly, in favor of things that are superficial and showy, that have no ultimate value. . . . I will say as a brother monk from the West to Eastern monks . . . the time is coming when you may face the same situation and your ancient traditions will stand you in good stead.[65]

Perhaps most alarming, however, is a marginal note left in one of Merton's last working notebooks kept while at his hermitage at Gethsemani. It is in this same notebook that Merton made his initial notations for what would become his article "The Wild Places":

The dreadful fact [is] that I was born into this world at the very moment when the whole thing came to a head[;] it is precisely in my lifetime that civilization has undergone this massive attack from within itself. My whole life is shaped by this. . . . It presses on the brain with a (near) darkness.[66]

Forty years after recording this observation, forty years after Merton's accidental death while visiting with monastic men and women from around the world, the "dreadful fact" of this "massive attack" continues to press in on our brains with ever-increasing darkness. Merton—and I think most of us would agree about this at least in part—had diagnosed the dilemma accurately and insightfully. He also sensed very deeply the almost desperate circumstances in which the technological/ecological crisis was and would continue to be played out. Nevertheless, he suggested no real solid programs or tactics for action. Perhaps Merton would have come to suggest something once he returned to Gethsemani. We will never know. It is, I suspect, the hope of everyone who contributed to, and is reading, this book that not only will further consciousness-raising occur but also some sort of preliminary steps may be broached toward some type of action—whether local or global, personal or communal—that we can begin to take in our own daily lives. Some of the most fundamental, and perhaps the most effective, of these actions are, for monks and contemplatives, already obvious.

I would like to give the final word not to Thomas Merton, but to another brother monk, Fr. Bruno Barnhart, a Camaldolese Benedictine of Big Sur, California. In his book *The Future of Wisdom: Toward a Rebirth of Sapiential Christianity*, Fr. Bruno sums up the life and work of Thomas Merton in this way:

> Roughly during the last decade of his life—Merton began to move back toward the modern world which he had left behind, particularly those thinkers and writers with whom he felt a great affinity. He was moving further into the country of imagination, and at the same time apparently discovering the wide ecumenical territory of the sapiential, in which he was able to rediscover everything that he loved. The sapiential world, in the new sense in which he was coming to conceive it, included the mystery of Christ and the archetypal contemplative East; but it also included everything of value that had been left outside the walls of his earlier theological enclosure, labeled "Toxic-Secular." Merton was awakening to a new Christian wisdom in which the immanent force of incarnation has awakened divinity within the human person in the active, creative mode. . . . Gradually the early Merton's Catholic and monastic triumphalism . . . gives way to a more sober experience of the life of faith and a deeper awareness of solidarity in the human condition. . . . This is the threshold of postmodernity, of the post-Western mind, of global consciousness and global participation at every level.[67]

Thomas Merton exhorts us to meet the sometimes horrific challenges, but at the same time to make fruitful use, of the unique situations that constitute our postmodern world. This is a call to journey into that wide ecumenical territory of the imagination and of the sapiential; to tap into the divine within each of us, allowing for an ever more profound sense of "solidarity in the human condition"; to recall, reinforce, and revive our own ancient traditions that will stand us in good stead as things around us grow ever more bizarre; to put on a global mind of participation at every level before it is too late and the darkness has covered us completely.

II

Buddhist and Christian Teaching on the World and Our Place in It

Religious Vision and Ethical Choices

Dependent Origination and the Causes and Conditions behind the Climate Crisis

Ajahn Punnadhammo

What can Buddhism contribute to our understanding of the environmental crisis we are facing today? I will attempt to consider briefly how the core teaching of dependent origination can be applied to an understanding of our global predicament.

One of the central axioms of Buddhist thought is the principle of causality. The short formula, occurring in several places in the Pali texts is "This being; that exists. Through the arising of this that arises. This not being, that does not exist; through the ceasing of this; that ceases."

This assertion may seem a truism, hardly worth stating, but taken in the context of ancient Indian philosophical discourse, it is a strong statement. It amounts to a declaration that events and objects in this universe arise due to causes and conditions and not otherwise—that is, not randomly or through the arbitrary will of a deity, as taught by other schools at that time.

This principle of causality underlies much of the Buddha's own teaching, as well as being a cornerstone of later Buddhist thought. When speaking about some positive or negative factor, the Buddha would often ask, "What is the cause, the condition, for the arising of this? What is the cause, the condition for its cessation?" The logical structure of his expositions was very often based on these chains of causality.

The most well-known and commonly cited example is the twelve stages of dependent origination. These stages are given as an explanation for "how this whole mass of suffering comes to be"—or, in other words, of *samsaric* existence: this mortal world of birth, death, and rebirth. There is no ultimate origin, in Buddhism, for *samsara*, which is conceived of as beginingless. So it is made clear that the twelve stages are to be seen as a dynamic ongoing process, not as a linear movement through historical time. Briefly stated, the twelve stages are given as ignorance, karmic action, consciousness, body and mind, the six senses, contact, feeling, craving, clinging, becoming, birth, and finally, old age and death.

It is not my intention here to stray from my topic and discuss this sequence in detail. It is a profound and complex subject that has spawned a vast and sometimes contentious literature involving several possible lines of interpretation. But for the benefit of those who may be new to this doctrine, what follows is a very concise summary explanation based on the most traditional reading.

Because beings are ignorant of ultimate truths, they act in the world in various ways, creating the seeds of karma. When they come to the end of their lifespan, these seeds are still present, needing to be expressed. This results in consciousness again arising in some state of being, for instance, a human womb. The consciousness in the womb, conditioned by its old karma, provides the guiding matrix for the unfolding of a new body-mind system. This new organism is equipped with the six senses—the five classical physical ones as well as the mind sense, which takes thought as an object. These six senses provide the opportunity for the being to make contact with the outer world. The various contacts are felt by the being as pleasant, unpleasant, or neutral, and this causes him or her to crave more of the pleasant ones, and to escape from the unpleasant ones. This craving is a very primitive impulse, but it matures into clinging, wherein the desire starts to become a "project." Plans are made and actions are taken, and this culminates in becoming. That is to say, the being recreates himself or herself as the possessor of the desired. This re-creation involves the accumulation of much fresh karmic debt, which again culminates in birth into the world. And birth always results in ageing and death. "Thus this whole mass of suffering comes to be."

One of the applications of this principle of dependent origination is in the explication of the Buddhist teaching of voidness or not-self. No entity or event in the universe can be conceived of as single and independent. Everything exists only by the action of prior and contemporary causes. We may naïvely conceive of ourselves as independent beings, but the atoms of our physical form are constantly exchanged with the outer world and the contents of our minds are filled with ideas and thoughts originating in other minds. There is no real self-substance (*svabhava*). One way this has been expressed is "nothing exists from its own side."

Later Buddhist thought elaborated these ideas considerably, particularly in the Mahayana tradition, with its great emphasis on the emptiness principle (*sunyata*). A corollary to the causal principle coined by the philosopher Nagarjuna states that "nothing arises without a cause, and nothing arises from a single cause." The linear form in which dependent origination was usually presented was supplemented with a multidimensional matrix of mutual dependence. The Hua Yen School especially developed this idea. In the *Avatamsatka Sutra* we find the metaphor of Indra's Net used to illustrate the complexity of mutual causation. In the palace of the god Indra there hangs a net, a complex three-dimensional weave. At each crossing of the threads there is a multifaceted jewel. In each facet of each jewel one can see the whole of the net being reflected, including all the other jewels in an infinite regress.

This complex and holistic vision of reality is in stark contrast to the way in which much of Western thought has, until recently, viewed the world. Modern science, beginning in the seventeenth century, has made great progress in understanding the world. It has done this largely by using a reductionist methodology of studying the various components of this world as independent, self-contained units. A process of intellectual analysis has broken down organisms into cells, and cells into organic molecules. Likewise in the physical sciences, the thrust of research has always been toward identifying and classifying more and more fundamental particles of matter.

This reductionist habit of thought has, without dispute, proved to be a powerful tool. But it is, in the last analysis, not an expression of reality but only a model of reality, useful in many contexts but misleading in others. After four hundred years the habit of reductionism, of missing the forest for the trees, is deeply ingrained in Western thought. It is not without significance that the one field of scientific inquiry that has had to transcend this habit, from the outset, is ecology, because it seeks to understand the interplay of living and nonliving systems on both a local and a planetary scale. So, reductionism is, I would suggest, an intellectual handicap in trying to find solutions to the climate crisis. Many of the proposed solutions are thought to be helpful only if they are considered in a limited, reductionist way. They may even be harmful when a more holistic, interdependent view is taken.

A prime example is the use of biofuels derived from Indian corn and other crops. Considered locally, they appear very positive. The carbon is recycled through a fast-growing plant; next year's corn takes up this year's exhaust. The long-cycle carbon bound up in petrochemicals can be left in the ground. However, when the full picture of the production of the crops, the transportation of the raw grain, the processing of the alcohol, and so on are taken into account, it is found that there is actually a huge net increase in energy consumption. What is more, with current agricultural practices even the use of fossil fuel is increased because the chemical inputs are largely derived from petrochemicals. And all of this is in addition to the food crisis that is already beginning as more and more cropland is diverted to biofuel production. This diversion has even resulted in the clearing of rainforest in Indonesia and elsewhere in order to cash in on the biofuel boom. Considered with all its causes and conditions, biofuels, far from being a solution, are an unmitigated environmental disaster.

Turning to the real theme of this chapter, what can Buddhism tell us about the causes and conditions of environmental degradation, which in the Buddha's time was not even considered a problem? For example, there is a passage in early Buddhist literature that compares the qualities of the Dhamma (Dharma) to those of the "Great Ocean," and states that the Dhamma is incorruptible, just as the Great Ocean: no matter what manner of rubbish is thrown into the ocean, it is too vast to be defiled. We would no longer consider this to be true. Our capacity for generating rubbish exceeds that of the ancient Indians by several orders of magnitude.

Although it would be vain to search for an explanation of climate change in terms of dependent origination, we can make a reasonable extrapolation by considering a parallel case. Here, the Buddha deals with another human problem that was known already in his time and from which we still suffer today, the problem of war. In the *Mahadukkhakkhanda Sutta (Sutra)* the Buddha says that "men strap on armor and shield and hack one another with swords, just for sensual desire." Thus, the desire to please the senses is said to be the underlying cause and condition of warfare. Put in modern terms, this would mean that the Buddha was proposing a theory of economic causation for international conflict. This is a view that is hard to refute; all, or at least almost all, cases of warfare can be explained in terms of struggle for resources such as land, water, or oil—that is, resources that we use to produce commodities that serve to satisfy our sense desires.

I would suggest the same ultimate cause underlies our environmental problems. In the language of dependent origination: Because we desire the pleasant feelings arising from sense contact we produce and consume products made from petrochemicals and produce carbon dioxide as a by-product. Or—to state it in a way more in line with the traditional formula—because of sense desire there arises consumerism, because of consumerism there arises commodity production, because of commodity production there arises resource extraction, because of resource extraction there arises greenhouse gas release, and because of greenhouse gas release there arises climate change. And thus this whole mass of suffering comes to be "on account of sense desire, just because of sense desire."

This identification of the cause points the way to the only possible solution. Most of the solutions so far proposed or implemented fall short or are, like biofuels, actually counterproductive. This is because they do not address the underlying cause. There is a widespread search for ways and means to satisfy our sensual desires without damage to the environment. This is ultimately a hopeless endeavor. The problem is not in this or that detail of our economy, but in its very basis. Modern society is absolutely profligate in its use of resources primarily because our value system is based on finding happiness through pleasing the senses. Our economists are still fixated on generating growth, on the production of more and better commodities designed to satisfy human sense desires.

The underlying problem is not the way we produce things, it is in the sheer volume of things we produce above and beyond what is needed to sustain physical health and well-being. The solution will be found not in seeking a different way of doing the same things, but in finding ways to do with less. For this to have any hope of working, it would require a radical change in our value system. We need to find ways to happiness that are not based on consuming resources. It may be here that religious and especially monastic traditions can make a contribution. Buddhism often speaks about finding our real happiness within. The Buddha praised *jhana* (meditative absorption) as "the blameless happiness divorced from the senses." Likewise, one of the virtues to be cultivated is *santutthi*, or contentment with little. Serving as an example of a lifestyle that offers fulfillment without frenzied consumption may be one of the most useful services that monastic communities, whatever their tradition, may be able to provide the world at this time of crisis.

Buddhism identifies three primal roots of all ill: greed, hatred, and delusion. If we can agree that greed for material objects to please the senses is the primary root of climate change, I think we can also identify delusion as a major secondary cause. One form this takes is the widespread denial of the problem. This late in the day, governments everywhere are debating carbon-emission targets that the climate scientists say are, even if they were implemented, far too little, far too late. Targets that would actually save the planet from catastrophe are dismissed as politically unrealistic, so the politicians pick numbers more to their liking out of thin air and news commentators earnestly debate them. Something is wrong with this picture.

Among the causes and conditions of this denial we can certainly identify wishful thinking and the shortsightedness dictated by four- or five-year election cycles. But I think there is something a little more fundamental at work as well. Our technological society has allowed us to become insulated and therefore alienated from the natural world. For the city-dweller in the developed world, electricity comes out of a wall socket, water comes out of a tap, heating fuel is piped in, and bodily wastes are flushed neatly away. Where any of this material comes from or goes to remains an abstraction. When you are required to pump your water by hand and carry it in buckets, you are naturally less inclined to be wasteful of it.

Most of humanity now lives in cities, and in an urban environment it is probably neither possible nor desirable to pursue a technological reversion. Medieval cities were loathsome, unhealthy places. We cannot do without our complex infrastructure. This said, urban planning for the future ought to reverse some of the trends of the last century and build cities for people and not for automobiles. And do we really need to consume huge amounts of electricity to try and turn night into day? During the big East Coast blackout of 2003, many young adult city-dwellers saw the Milky Way for the first time in their lives.

I wonder about the spiritual effect of blotting out the stars. However, the amount that can be done toward overcoming our alienation from nature by physical changes is limited. Here, too, the fundamental shift must be a spiritual one.

So, besides becoming less greedy, people need to somehow become more in tune with their place in the natural world, to reconnect with the interdependent web of which they are inescapably a part. Reducing greed and reconnecting to the interdependent world in which we live would reverse several centuries of development. The whole thrust of our culture and technology has been to insulate us from the discomforts and deprivations of nature and to provide us with more and better artificial amusements. These trends go back at least to the Enlightenment, and it is hard to see how they can be reversed with anything short of a spiritual revolution. Or perhaps we should say, a counterrevolution, a return to the ethos of a simpler time.

Our civilization has, without dispute, made a brilliant career during these last four or five centuries. We have conquered space and time, the infirmities of the body, and the vagaries of nature to an extent unknown before. But it has not been without a cost, and it seems the bill is coming due. Our material enrichment has been bought at the cost of a spiritual impoverishment. The materialist and reductionist habits of mind that have made science and technology possible have also alienated us from the natural world and from our own deepest nature. As a culture, we have lost touch with both the organic and the numinous. These powerful forces cannot be denied forever.

For all these reasons, I would suggest that we ought to be very skeptical of any technological fix to our problem. The manifestation of the problem may be technological, but the underlying causes and conditions are a spiritual malaise, and, until that is addressed, the problem will not go away.

The World as Created, Fallen, and Redeemed

Fr. James Wiseman, OSB

Back in the summer of 1995, three other Benedictines and I had the opportunity to spend five weeks in Tibet and North India, mainly to visit Buddhist sites and engage in dialogue with Tibetan monks and nuns. I well remember how on one occasion at a monastery in India I had just begun a brief presentation on some basic Christian doctrines when, as soon as I mentioned our belief in a creator God, many of the Tibetan monks in the audience started giggling. They certainly didn't intend to be offensive, but the very idea of a creator of the universe seemed to them so preposterous that they inevitably found it humorous. I am actually grateful for their response, for it prevents me from blithely assuming that Buddhists and Christians are merely saying the same thing in different words. Indeed, some Buddhist authors, both classical and modern, have written severe critiques of the doctrine of a Creator God. Whether or not there is a possibility of bridging the gap between our two traditions on this point—as has been suggested in one recent book—is something that we could discuss.[1] I'll broach one way of possibly building such a bridge at the end of this chapter, but first I want to discuss as briefly and as accurately as possible what the Christian doctrine is.

In order to give a particularly clear example of what Christians mean by creation as brought about and preserved in being by God, let me present another anecdote, this one from the life of one of the most prominent Catholic theologians of the past fifty years. By the time Avery Dulles graduated from a New England prep school in the spring of 1936, he was a thoroughgoing materialist, holding that every notion of God was merely an invention of the human mind to explain things that could otherwise not be accounted for. He entered Harvard College that fall, still ensconced in what he called a "cold, amoral world . . . governed only by chance and by the selfish actions of human persons engaged in the cruel quest for pleasure."[2] Then, one afternoon early in the spring semester of his sophomore year, as he was reading a chapter of Augustine's *City of God* in Widener Library, something remarkable occurred. Here is how he later described what happened:

> On an impulse I closed the book; I was irresistibly prompted to go out into the open air. It was a bleak rainy day, rather warm for the time of year. The slush of melting snow formed a deep mud along the banks of the River Charles, which I followed down toward Boston. . . . As I wandered aimlessly, something impelled me to look contemplatively at a young tree. On its frail, supple branches were young buds attending eagerly the spring which was at hand. While my eye rested on them the thought came to me suddenly, with all the strength and novelty of a revelation, that these little buds in their innocence and meekness followed a rule, a law of which I as yet knew nothing. How could it be, I asked, that this delicate tree sprang up and developed and that all the enormous complexity of its cellular operations combined together to make it grow erectly and bring forth leaves and blossoms? The answer, the trite answer of the schools, was new to me: that its actions were ordered to an end by the only power capable of adapting means to ends—intelligence—and that the very fact that this intelligence worked toward an end implied purposiveness—in other words, a will. . . . Mind, then, not matter, was at the origin of all things. Or rather not so much the "mind" of [the

Greek philosopher] Anaxagoras as a Person of Whom I had had no previous intuition.

Nor were the operations of this Person confined to flowers and foliage. The harmonious motions of the stars, the distribution of the elements, and the obedience of matter to fixed laws were manifestations of the same will and plan. Looking, then, into myself, I beheld energies coursing through the human person, the greater part of them beyond the realm of consciousness, tending constantly to preserve, to nourish, and to restore the weary body and soul. These forces were not of our own making . . . yet they had from their inception a legitimacy which was conferred upon them by Another—the same as Him Who moved the stars and made the lilacs bloom. . . .

. . . As I turned home that evening, the darkness closing round, I was conscious that I had discovered something which would introduce me to a new life, set off by a sharp hiatus from the past.

That night, for the first time in years, I prayed. I knelt down in the chill blackness at my bedside, as my mother had taught me to do when I was a little boy, and attempted to raise my heart and mind toward Him of Whose presence and power I had become so unexpectedly aware.[3]

Dulles goes on to say that this event—which was the beginning of his conversion, even though he did not become a Catholic until he started law school a few years later—did not rest on some sort of rational proof. In his words, "My own acceptance of the existence of God rested on something more like an intuition. It was as though I had seen, at least for an instant, the divine power at work, infusing the whole universe with goodness and being. . . . I recorded it as best I can."[4]

This well-known theologian, who was raised to the rank of cardinal by Pope John Paul II a few years ago, and who died in 2008, just after retiring from an endowed chair in the department of theology at Fordham University, would be the first to admit that his experience along the banks of the River Charles held but a glimmer of the rich doctrine of creation and divine providence that has developed over the centuries. So, too, in my own short chapter I can do no more than point to some of the most salient aspects of this doctrine.

To begin, consider the opening verses of the first book of the Bible: "In the beginning when God created the heavens and the earth, the earth was a formless void and darkness covered the face of the deep, while a wind from God swept over the face of the waters. Then God said, 'Let there be light'; and there was light" (Gen. 1:1–3; NRSV translation). In the Bible, the Hebrew word that is here translated as "created" is regularly used of God alone, as distinct from another verb that could be translated as "made" and that applies also to human activity. When we humans "make" something, there is always some material at hand out of which we fashion whatever we intend. God, however, creates merely by his word, as is abundantly clear by the frequently repeated phrase "And God said" throughout this first chapter of the Book of Genesis. By the end of the second century BCE, what later Christian theologians called *creatio ex nihilo* ("creation out of nothing") was expressed by the Jewish author of the Second Book of Maccabees in the following words: "Look at the heaven and the earth and see everything that is in them, and recognize that God did not make them out of things that existed. And in the same way the human race came into being" (2 Macc. 7:28).

That God created merely by his word eventually had major implications for Christian theology. The Fourth Gospel, commonly called the Gospel according to John, significantly begins in a way that clearly reflects the opening verse of the Book of Genesis. The evangelist writes: "In the beginning was the Word," and then proceeds to say that "the Word was with God, and the Word was God. He was in the beginning with God. All things came into being through him, and without him not one thing came into being" (John 1:1–3). The prologue to the Fourth Gospel goes on to say that this divine Word became flesh in Jesus of Nazareth and lived among us. One finds here the seeds of a Trinitarian understanding of creation: in Christian terms, God the Father creates though the Word, otherwise called the Son of God, incarnate in Jesus the Christ. The one whom Christians call the third person of the Trinity, the Holy Spirit, is likewise involved in creation. When the Book of Genesis says that in the beginning "a wind from God swept over the face of the waters," the Hebrew word for "wind" could just as well be translated as "breath" or "spirit." One of the longest and most beautiful of the Psalms, Psalm 104, reflects this understanding when it says of living creatures: "These all look to you to give them their food in due season; . . . When you send forth your spirit, they are created; and you renew the face of the earth" (104:27, 30). It was natural and even inevitable for Christians to understand such a verse as referring to the Holy Spirit. For this reason, creation is understood to be the work of the entire Godhead: Father, Son, and Holy Spirit.

A question worth pondering, at least briefly, is whether such creation implies a beginning in (or better, "with") time. Early Christian theologians like Irenaeus of Lyons in the second century and Augustine of Hippo in the fourth certainly thought so, and in the Middle Ages the Franciscan theologian Bonaventure even held that one could prove philosophically that the world had a beginning in time. However, his still more influential contemporary Thomas Aquinas disagreed. Noting that in the most fundamental sense creation refers to a relationship of utter dependence on God even if this relationship is from all eternity, Aquinas taught that it is only by revelation that we can know that the world did not always exist. According to him, such revelation was manifest in the opening words of the Bible, the Latin text that he used being literally translated as "In the beginning God created heaven and earth." Some prominent theologians today, such as Jürgen Moltmann and Ted Peters, agree on this point, the latter writing that to reduce the doctrine of creation "to a vague commitment about the dependence of the world upon God . . . simply moves the matter to a higher level of abstraction. We still need to ask: just what does it mean for the world to owe its existence to God? One sensible answer is this: had God not acted to bring the space-time world into existence, there would be only nothing."[5] Other theologians, how-ever, are of a different mind. For example, Keith Ward writes that the notion that the universe had a beginning "was usually accepted because of a particular reading of Genesis 1. The doctrine of creation *ex nihilo* simply maintains that there is nothing other than God from which the universe is made, and that the universe is other than God and wholly dependent upon God for its existence."[6]

Despite disagreement on that particular point, there is a solid consensus among Christians that creation is fundamentally good, even as God is goodness itself. Six times in the opening chapter of the Book of Genesis we read that after God created one or another thing, "God saw that it was good," while in the final verse of that chapter this phrase is even intensified: "God saw everything that he had made, and indeed, it was very good" (Gen. 1:31). Often in the course of Christian history saintly writers have exulted over this fact, and not only with respect to what are usually considered the more momentous signs of God's love. The fourth-century Syrian poet and hymnist St. Ephrem once composed some beautiful lines expressing his wonder and gratitude for even the smallest tokens of God's goodness:

> Let us see those things that He does for us every day!
> How many tastes for the mouth! How many beauties for the
>   eye!
> How many melodies for the ear! How many scents for the
>   nostrils!
> Who is sufficient in comparison to the goodness of these
>   little things?
> Who is able to make thousands of remunerations in a day?[7]

Nine centuries later St. Francis of Assisi echoed something of St. Ephrem's delight in the goodness of creation, above all in his *Canticle of Brother Sun*, part of which reads as follows:

> Praised be You, my Lord, with all your creatures,
> especially Sir Brother Sun,
> Who is the day and through whom You give us light.
> And he is beautiful and radiant with great splendor;
> and bears a likeness of You, Most High One.
> Praised be You, my Lord, through Sister Moon and the stars,
> in heaven You formed them clear and precious and
>   beautiful.[8]

Much of what I have said up to now refers to what is sometimes called "original creation," that is, to God's creating "in the beginning"; but this ought never to be understood apart from "ongoing creation" (*creatio continua*), that is, God's providentially holding everything in existence. Perhaps no one has expressed this in such memorable imagery as the fourteenth-century Englishwoman Julian of Norwich, whose book of *Showings* has become enormously popular in recent decades. In one of the best-known passages from her work, Julian writes that

> our good Lord showed a spiritual sight of his familiar love. I saw that he is to us everything which is good and comforting for our help.... And so in this sight I saw that he is everything which is good, as I understand.
>   And in this he showed me something small, no bigger than a hazelnut, lying in the palm of my hand, as it seemed to me, and it was as round as a ball. I looked at it with the eye of my understanding and thought: What can this be? I was amazed that it could last, for I thought that because of its littleness it would suddenly have fallen into nothing. And

> I was answered in my understanding: It lasts and always will,
> because God loves it; and thus everything has being through
> the love of God.[9]

Third, in addition to original creation and ongoing creation, there
is our Christian belief in a "new creation" (*creatio nova*). Both Christians and Buddhists recognize that there is suffering and incompleteness in the world, even if our respective understandings of the origin
of suffering are not exactly the same. For Christians, at least much of
what is unsatisfactory about our life is due to that self-centered turning away from God that we call "sin." Already St. Paul, in a well-known
passage from his Letter to the Romans, sensed that sin has affected
not only us human beings who perpetrate it but also the very world in
which we live. In his words,

> I consider that the sufferings of this present time are not
> worth comparing with the glory about to be revealed to us.
> For the creation waits with eager longing for the revealing of
> the children of God; for the creation was subjected to futility,
> not of its own will but by the will of the one who subjected it,
> in hope that the creation itself will be set free from its bond-
> age to decay and will obtain the freedom of the glory of the
> children of God. (Rom. 8:18–21)

I will be the first to admit that a passage like that is open to various interpretations. Nowadays most scientists believe that after some
incalculable number of years the forces of entropy will lead the entire
universe to devolve into a state of low-grade radiation with a tem-
perature approaching absolute zero, unable to support any kind of
life. Some theologians have found that scenario so troubling that
they interpret Paul's words in Romans, along with similar passages
in the Book of Isaiah about "a new heavens and a new earth" (Isa.
65:17), in a very literal sense as portending an eventual, momentous

renewal or redemption of all creation. I myself am far more cautious in this regard. As I have written elsewhere, "One of the most constant themes in the spiritual teaching of the world's religious traditions is that human beings ought not to cling to possessions of one sort or another and that things will in fact normally be much more appreciated and enjoyed if one does not cling to them or yearn for them to have a permanence that is not appropriate."[10] This surely holds not just for objects in our immediate vicinity but for the universe as a whole. As William Blake wrote in his short poem "Eternity,"

> He who binds to himself a joy
> Does the winged life destroy;
> But he who kisses the joy as it flies
> Lives in eternity's sun rise.

As I approach the end of my chapter, there are two further issues that should be addressed. The first is whether there is something in Christian doctrine that tends to make Christians ecologically irresponsible. Even those Christians who have written most ardently about the goodness of creation recognized that it is not ultimate, and many of them have used expressions that do denigrate the world around us. Julian of Norwich, immediately after speaking of God as creator, protector, and lover of all that God has made, writes: "God wishes to be known, and it pleases him that we should rest in him; for everything which is beneath him is not sufficient for us. And this is the reason why no soul is at rest until it has despised as nothing all things which are created."[11] This is the kind of language that led Karl Marx to speak of religion as "the opium of the people," people yearning for "pie in the sky by and by" while despising material reality. A related criticism is that the Christian tradition in particular is largely responsible for the exploitation of nature, as famously argued by Professor Lynn White, Jr., in an often-anthologized article first published in 1967.[12] White claimed that "in Antiquity every tree, every spring, every stream, every hill had its own *genius loci*, its guardian spirit. . . . Before one cut a tree, mined a mountain, or dammed a brook, it was important to placate the spirit in charge of that particular situation, and to keep it placated. By destroying pagan animism, Christianity made it possible to exploit nature in a mood of indifference to the feelings of natural objects."[13] Still others have asserted that when God, in the first chapter of Genesis, tells humans to "fill the earth and subdue it; and have dominion over the fish of the sea and over the birds of the air and over every living thing that moves upon the earth" (Gen. 1:28), this command gives us carte blanche to treat the world around us in any way that seems to be for our benefit.

What are we to make of such charges? First, there has unquestionably been a world-denying quality in many expressions of Christian spirituality, though this is so much less the case today that some feel the pendulum has swung too far in the opposite direction. With regard to White's main point, it is crucial to recognize that if the Judeo-Christian tradition rejected the notion that every natural object had its own *genius loci*, there is a real sense in which Judaism and Christianity are themselves animistic. When the 104th Psalm says that God's spirit "renews the face of the earth" (v. 30) and the Book of Wisdom affirms that "the spirit of the Lord has filled the world" (1:7), this implies that the multifarious guardian spirits of ancient animism have given way to a single, omnipresent Spirit abiding in every creature. It was this awareness that led a mystic such as the Jesuit scientist Pierre Teilhard de Chardin to pray to God in the following words: "Blazing Spirit, Fire, personal, super-substantial, . . . be pleased yet once again to come down and breathe a soul into the newly formed, fragile film of matter with which this day the world is to be freshly clothed."[14] Moreover, Teilhard de Chardin and many others, including St. Francis of Assisi, the patron saint of ecologists, have sensed the kinship that humans have with all other creatures, a kinship that led Francis to speak of Brother Sun and Sister Moon, Brother Wolf and Sister Water, even as contemporary science has shown us that we share our DNA, to one degree or another, with every living being on earth. As Jürgen Moltmann writes in his book *God in Creation*, "If the Holy Spirit is poured out on the whole creation, then [the Spirit] creates the community of all created things with God and with each other, making it that fellowship of creation in which all created things communicate with one another and with God, each in its own way."[15] In the simplest terms, this means that we humans are not above nature but are part of nature and that Christians, no less than Buddhists, can rightly speak of a certain interdependence of everything on earth. Some have indeed interpreted the biblical charge to "subdue" the earth and "have dominion" over other creatures in a way that justifies exploitation, but the contemporary environmental crisis surely stems primarily either from human greed or the direst need and not from some scriptural text. After all, there are regions on earth that have suffered tremendous environmental devastation and yet have scarcely been touched by the Judeo-Christian tradition. Our call as human beings, regardless of our particular religious tradition, is to be responsible stewards, mindful of our kinship with other creatures and of our responsibility to care for them and for the earth itself with a love that reflects what we Christians believe to be God's own love for all creation. The practical challenge is to allow this awareness to influence the way we actually live on our fragile planet.

Finally, there is a point I alluded to earlier: Is the Christian understanding of creation ineluctably at odds with Buddhist teaching? An entire book could be devoted to this topic, not least because there are different emphases within various schools of Christian thought and also within Buddhism. It is worth noting, however, that for a great theologian such as Thomas Aquinas the world, whether or not it had a beginning, exists because of God, and "ultimately, this 'because of' needs to be understood as a 'final cause' . . . that is, as a *telos*."[16] In other words, everything in the cosmos exists for the reason or for the purpose of moving toward this ultimate divine goal. When one considers that in Buddhist teaching all sentient beings have an inclination toward nirvana, there does appear a certain parallelism that deserves further reflection and investigation. To be sure, the God whom Christians worship is primarily described in personal terms whereas nirvana is not, but the difference is not absolute. Christian thinkers such as Paul Tillich and Henri Le Saux have written eloquently of an impersonal aspect to the Godhead, while the Japanese Buddhist monk Shinran, who died in 1263 CE, claimed that "the utmost we can say about ultimate reality before admitting its ultimate ineffability is that, for us, the ultimate is like an infinitely compassionate father/mother."[17] Regardless of whether or not we conclude that the Buddhist and Christian approaches to the question of creation are compatible, we can surely agree with Perry Schmidt-Leukel when he writes:

> Both Christians and Buddhists could challenge and encourage one another to practice an attitude [toward the world] which combines loving involvement with selfless detachment. Buddhists may remind Christians that creation is not an end in itself, but has its goal in redemption, and Christians may remind Buddhists that the path to salvation and the existence in salvation are acted out here, in communion with all others, and nowhere else.[18]

III

Monastic Rules on the World
and Our Life in It

*Bringing New Awareness to
Ancient Yet Living Documents*

The Monastic Rules of Theravada and Mahayana Buddhism

*The Bhikshu Pattimokha and the
Ten Major and Forty-eight Minor
Bodhisattva Precepts from the
Net of Brahma (Brahmajmala) Sutra*

Rev. Heng Sure, PhD

*O Monks, indeed, the entire world is burning;
all things are burning. Monks![1]*

Often after hours at the computer my eyeballs feel dry and irritated. Apparently the itching and burning has something to do with hours of staring at the monitor, which leads to fewer eyeblinks, which leads to dehydration of the surface of the eyeball. To solve the problem I must step away from the machine, or turn it off, and cool off the flaming, flickering pixelated images that burn patterns of light into my sensitive eyeballs.

I can easily find relief from my burning eyes by shutting down the computer. In the Buddha's third teaching, called the *Fire Sutta*, he says that not only the eyes but all the senses are on fire. He shifts the cause of the discomfort from external to internal. He says that it's not the world, rather, "the senses are on fire." Then the Buddha goes on to specify: "The eyes are on fire. The objects of sight are on fire, the eye consciousness is on fire . . . ." and so on through eighteen senses,

sense-objects, and sense consciousnesses. When seen through burning senses, the world itself looks to be on fire. Then he gives the solution to the burning of the senses: the moral precepts. Why follow the
precepts and live a wholesome life? Because to do so puts out the fires
of the senses. Why be good? Because being good makes the world a
better place. Sounds simplistic, but it's been the monastic community's method to living responsibly in the environment for centuries.

In the *Flower Adornment Sutra*, the Buddha says, "The perfection
of morality (*sila paramita*) lies in its ability to eradicate the fires of all
afflictions." In other words, extinguishing the fires of afflictions con-
stitutes the highest expression of morality. Thus the precepts of the
monastic rule are the antidote to the burning of the senses. By extension, these precepts are the antidote to the fires of the world, by infer-
ence the antidote to the warming of the climate worldwide. From the
Buddha's perspective, a moral code functions to eradicate the burning
sensation that afflicts the senses and the mind as well as the harmful
warming of the planet.

This leads us to our topic: the approach toward climate change
contained in teachings embedded within the Buddhist Monastic precept codes, and from those codes, making visible the centuries-old
compassionate relationship between monastic communities and the
natural world.

I am collating two Buddhist rules, that of the Theravada tradition
(the code known as the *Patimokkha*) as well as that of the Mahayana
(known as the *Pratimoksha*). *Pratimoksha* means "leading to liberation." The code used by the Theravada tradition stems from Pali language recensions, and the Mahayana tradition from Sanskrit language
recensions. All Buddhist monastic traditions honor the *Pratimoksha*
rules, which is a list of monastic precepts meant to be recited every
two weeks. In addition, the Mahayana tradition uniquely honors an
additional monastic code known as the *Bodhisattva* Precepts (found
in the *Brahma Net [Brahmajmala] Sutra*).

Both traditions agree that the *bhikshu* (*bhikkhu*) and *bhikshuni*

(*bhikkuni*) precepts were laid out one by one, as the monks and nuns
went astray. As his disciples behaved in ways that led away from liberation, the Buddha would say, "*Bhikkhus!* Restrain this behavior
because it will hinder progress on your spiritual path." Over time the
sangha compiled the 227 Theravada precepts, the 250 Mahayana precepts, and the 348 *bhikshuni* precepts into the Pratimoksha codes. I
have referred to all three codes, as well as the *Bodhisattva* Precepts in
researching this topic.

In both Buddhist and Christian monastic rules there are relatively
few specific environmental references as we would define them today.
Why is this so? One possible reason might be because our monastic traditions—going back 2,550 years for Buddhists and 1,500 years
for Christians—were embedded in a worldview very different from
twenty-first-century worldviews. I suspect that the sangha community and the Christian cenobites for whom these rules were spoken
lived holistically in nature: they never imagined life could be broken
from the environment. They were likely so immersed in the natural
world, their lives were so inextricably tied to the environment, that
all teachings implicitly applied to the natural world and to its human
inhabitants as one, not two. There was simply no other world in play;
the environment did not require a special name. Ecological sanity did
not have to be pointed out; that we live as one with our natural surroundings was simply a given.

Since Buddhist monastic texts do not explicitly address these concerns, I will look at the monastic practices that arise from the *Pratimoksha* rules in order to glean the values and the perspectives that
created a cohesive and consistent approach to the environment in
Buddhist monastic communities. I will attempt to show how those
precepts serve as an interface to our lives in the world, engaged in the
environment. I will read these texts and frame our methodology as if
the Buddha were an environmentalist concerned with preserving habitat; saving species from extinction; limiting population; coping with
toxic air, dwindling water, arid land, melting ice, deadly unseasonal

storms; and more importantly, as if he were addressing pervasive corporate greed in an industrialized society and an unhealthy populace polarized between morbid obesity and grinding scarcity.

This hermeneutic is applicable to the present time, because the guidelines of the precepts and rules of deportment from the earliest days of the sangha to the present are still with us, after thousands of years of continuous usage. We have sources, but we now have to examine them in the light of the environmental concerns that face us today. We will reconstruct an environmental perspective from the various precepts that have come down to us: in the Mahayana tradition, the *Dharmagupta*, also known as the "Four Part *Vinaya*"; in the Theravada tradition, which uses the Pali *Vinaya*; and in the Tibetan tradition, which uses the *Mulavarvastivada Vinaya*. Holding these Buddhist monastic precepts affect the environment directly in that they function as an interface. They are tools and guidelines to facilitate a monk's resolve to live the holy life and still make skillful decisions about the situations that he or she encounters in both the inner and outer worlds. In some cases monks choose to withdraw from the world, in others to remain in contact while transcending the world. Finally, there are monastics who enter the world and from there help living beings cross over; this would be a *bodhisattva* resolve. In any case, the rules allow one to engage the world without "leaving the Path"—that is, I believe that monastic rules specify an interface for skillful living on the planet.

How do the codes help us live skillfully? The *Pratimoksha* codes arise to guide monks and nuns toward harmless, compassionate engagement with the world, using virtuous behavior and wise expedient means.

I identify three main themes from the *Pratimokshas* that underlie the specific precepts.

First among these views is the idea that one who follows the monastic rule lives simply and without greed. Beyond a doubt, greed is the ruling ethos of our global marketplace culture. In this marketplace world—the culture in which we live our monastic lives—more is good and new is best.

The monastic rule celebrates human life in the world without honoring greed. Monks say, "There is an alternative worldview that functions without insatiable greed, a worldview that has sustained our lives for centuries, a view that is thriving at the present." That worldview emphasizes moderation instead of excess, the Middle Way instead of extremes, and sufficiency instead of life-denying scarcity.

Second is the emphasis on *ahimsa*, a Sanskrit word that means "not harming," or "nonviolence." The basic idea is that there is almost always a choice available, a way to live skillfully that is not at some fellow creature's expense. *Ahimsa* is an important hallmark of Buddhist monastic codes.

Third is "interdependence," the foundational idea that places our human lives on the planet back into an animated world, rejecting the alienation, sterility, and life-denying airlessness of the industrial, mechanized world. The monastic codes give us a humanity that is not broken from nature but is interdependent with it. The *Pratimoksha* rules take into account the presence of ghosts, ancestors, spirits, seasons, plants, and animals, and they stitch humanity back into the fabric of life instead of carelessly authorizing or providing religious sanction for humanity to bloat and consume or destroy the rest. We humans with our machines are the only species that has become a force of nature in itself. A word we propose cautiously to describe this view is "non-anthropocentricity," meaning that humans are a part of rather than the center of the universe.

Let us now look more closely at these three underlying themes of the *Pratimoksha* codes in Buddhism to see how they guide our relationship to the world in which we live today.

Monks have always lived simply, but that does not imply bitter compromises with scarcity. Instead they celebrate sufficiency—joyful, even sacred sufficiency. Monks' rules celebrate contentment with and gratitude for sufficiency. Monks do not survive by competing with everybody else for their slice of a dwindling pie of resources. They believe that if you live mindfully, carefully, avoid extremes and celebrate moderation, there is plenty. Gratitude for that sufficiency makes life joyful. Living simply, with contentment instead of greed, is a hallmark of monastic codes East and West.

The Buddha said that greed, hatred, and delusion are three poisons. Of the ten evil deeds, three of them are evils done by the mind. Greed is the foremost of those evils. Can you say it more strongly? Greed poisons the mind. When you take poison you get sick. Advertising in the marketplace tries to convince us that greed is best, is essential to our lives. Not only do monks not honor greed in their rule, they also do not make satisfying greed a guiding ethos in their daily lives. And yet monastic orders still thrive. This Middle Way is a key theme in the *Pratimokshas* that the Buddha taught, and it is central in Benedict's Rule as well. For us to point this out might be considered a blessing for our culture. The monastic emphasis on sufficiency may become a saving alternative when fossil fuels are no longer readily available.

Moderation: knowing when to stop. The Buddha said, "Happiness results from contentment, and fewness of desires." Since greed is a poison, practicing contentment counteracts greed. The practice of resting content and grateful with just enough arises from knowing sufficiency. This idea is significantly different from frugality and is the opposite of a worldview based on scarcity. As mentioned above, scarcity is the idea that everybody is struggling for a share of the same pie. In this view, since there is only so much to go around, scarcity leads inevitably to contention and competition. The monk's vision is based on a radically different view, the notion that sharing, reducing desires, and resting content with moderate needs are the sources of happiness.

A verse from the Chinese tradition says, "If you can be content, you will always be happy. If you can be patient, your heart will know peace." The Chinese characters tell their own story; their literal meaning is: "Know sufficiency, always happy. Able to be patient, spontaneously at peace." These are monastic virtues that monks exemplify with every meal. At the same time, they are lessons that can speak easily to the culture at large. Making do with sufficient material goods allows space for more spirit, more nourishment for the heart, more joy, and more satisfaction in life. If we can preserve this perspective for humanity it can become the larger gift of our encounter.

The second underlying perspective is *ahimsa,* the Sanskrit word that means nonharming and also nonviolence or harmlessness. A commitment to not harming, to living blamelessly, is noble, and also central to our monastic vocation. Clearly this view is embedded in both *Pratimoksha* codes, in various injunctions not to kill, not to light fires on open ground, not to dig the earth, to liberate beings when you witness their peril, and not to eat meat. This principle signals the unambiguous presence of ecological concerns in the Buddha's restraints for the sangha. Reverence for life means that many, but not all, monks have from the outset enjoyed plant-based diets instead of meat-based diets. Research is appearing every month to testify that removing meat from one's diet does more to reduce one's carbon footprint than buying a hybrid vehicle. Livestock are responsible for more harmful gases than internal combustion engines.

By and large, monastic kitchens have been vegetarian friendly, if not completely vegetarian. Many people are surprised to learn that Buddhist communities worldwide are not entirely vegetarian, with the exception of the Chinese and Vietnamese traditions. Why is that? Most Theravada monks still derive their daily meal from alms donated by lay householders; they accept what they are given. Tibetans traditionally lived at altitudes that did not permit the growing of grains and gardens. But even these culturally determined customs are changing in light of the global exchange of information and awareness of environmental realities. As lay donors wake up to the benefits of harmless, plant-based eating, monks' diets will follow suit.

That monks have traditionally avoided participating in the armed forces and military combat is also a significant part of *ahimsa.* The *Pratimoksha* forbids monks from taking up arms, or even from performing as a military envoy for a country. Monks may not visit battlefields or places of armed combat. The caution here is perhaps that armies might take advantage of a monk's noncombatant status to employ him or her as a messenger to benefit one side or another of the conflict.

The third value is interdependence and reanimating our interdependent relationship with all things. In Indra's Net, Buddhist commentarial literature describes a net of interlaced pearls cunningly contrived so that the totality of the net appears by reflection in each and every single pearl. In one, you see all. The contemplation of Indra's Net gives us a striking image of interdependence. It models a world set back on its foundations of premodern but globally connected values.

Now, in terms of interdependence, there is a notion in the *Pratimoksha* called "same body, great compassion." I feel kindred to all beings with whom I share an identical physical makeup and a single nature. Earth, air, fire, and water make up the body, and inside we share one identical, awakened nature. The earth element makes up the teeth, bones, tendons, and skin, and we share them with all mammals, invertebrates, and insects. We share the same air: heart, lungs, arteries, skin pores, and mouth. We share fire: for humans, 98.6 degrees Fahrenheit; for fish a little less. Without that fire, you die. And then there is water, which makes up over 80 percent of our bodies: blood, tears, saliva, and so on. From the Buddha's perspective, this is the way things are. This is nature and this is us.

My tradition, the Chinese Chan and Pure Land Schools, shares with our Thai Forest Tradition neighbors the cultural identity of "High Church Buddhists." When you come into the Berkeley Monastery there are lots of images of *bodhisattvas*, Dharma protectors, *arhats*, and dragons. The "Protestant Buddhists" tend to have a problem with that. New meditators who only know Zen, or Vipassana psychotherapists who met their Buddhism in the West, where it is shorn of its animistic Asian culture, react with surprise, even dismay. "What are you doing with all these images everywhere? I've never seen so many dragons in one place before."

The Buddha Dharma that came from Asia in the sutras and in the *Pratimoksha* is a world full of gods, dragons, and spiritual pantheons of animated and invisible creatures of all kinds. Sutras tell us that every Dharma gathering attracts an eightfold pantheon of *devas*, dragons, *yakshas*, *asuras*, *gandharvas*, *garudas*, *nagas*, demons, and fairies of all descriptions. The sutras describe the Buddha's purview, which includes countless living beings in worlds that exist within worlds. This Buddhist connection with the realms of spirit is confirmed by indigenous peoples the world round—premodern, earth-based peoples—who call the earth Pachamama, Mother Earth, Gaia, the Earth Household. They find the world a miraculous place of wonder, of terror, and most of all, of sentient spirit.

In their actual practices, monastic communities East and West inhabit the premodern world more than the scientific, linear, reductionist, postmodern world. I think most monasteries are closer to the Pachamama view of Mother Earth in their day-to-day practices. In this view, humanity is part of, and not apart from, kinship with all creatures. We are knit into and inextricably related to all other species. Our role as humans is to stay humble and reverent, not to waste, to be grateful and wise in our sharing and stewardship of resources, and to show compassion to other neighboring species who inhabit this planet with us. The Buddha in the sutras describes the earth as a community to be lived in harmoniously and wisely, not as a commodity to be exploited and consumed by the strongest and most ruthless.

To put into practice the views outlined here reanimates nature in our daily lives. We move one step closer to a respectful relationship with the resources that we usually only exploit. This lesson is primary in reevaluating the contribution monastic communities make toward global healing. In his updated "An Inconvenient Truth" lecture before the audience at the TED conference,[2] Nobel Laureate Al Gore says that humanity's capacity for greed is the primary cause of our current climate crisis.

The Buddha called greed a poison of the mind, and said essentially that both the destruction and the healing of the world is done in a single thought. The mind purged of greed opens the road to awakening. The mind filled with greed poisons the earth and creates the potential for affliction and suffering for all its inhabitants equally. You don't flush greed away; you transform it, transmute it by generosity and by giving.

In pointing to the monk's world, where nature is full of spirit and our lives resemble a premodern, indigenous culture's interdependent, animated worldview, I am not advocating a retreat to a mythical Golden Age of blissful innocence, an Eden before the temptation. Instead I am suggesting that we follow the Buddha's insistence on seeing things as they are—that we follow the wisdom of earth-based peoples who have always known that nature is one texture, one fabric, and that humanity is knit into it inextricably. We are all familiar with the famous, life-changing photograph of Planet Earth, taken from the moon. The year was 1969 and the photo came to be known as "earthrise." Once we saw that photograph, things were different. We saw the limits. We saw the finite quality of our home, our Earth Household. We noticed that close by our planet there is nothing but inky-black space.

Once we've seen the reality of our finite family of living beings spinning on the tiny blue marble of our planet in a vast, empty, infinite universe, there is no turning back to an isolated, self-interested, tribal view of life as a struggle for survival. We need to expand that view—incorporating the monastic wisdom and compassion that asks us to evolve, to step back from the feverish dream of the competitive marketplace to a premodern person's awe and appreciation of the interrelated power of the natural world—but with a global concern for all beings as one, large body, one interrelated, sentient family. We need to combine premodern wonder with a global ethical sense.

A monastic premodern lifestyle that includes a heartfelt connection with the earth and all its living beings can be a significant, healing gift from the monks to a world of weary, discouraged souls who have very little hope of finding a workable alternative view in the town square of our postmodern culture.

On October 3, 2003, at the dedication of the new technology center at the library of the Graduate Theological Union, University of California Berkeley's neighboring seminary, I offered the following prayer:

> Let us first invoke Indra's Net, the interlacing net of pearls, which in the Buddhist Pantheon is said to adorn the heavenly palace of Shakra Devanam Indra, lord of the "Heaven of the Thirty-three Gods." The net contains an infinite number of perfect, transparent pearls. Each pearl perfectly reflects the totality of pearls. In each pearl one can see all the pearls, and the entire network of pearls is gathered back by a single perfect pearl.
>
> May the electronic tools we use in the technology center reflect the totality of the spirit in the same way. May every micro-circuit that sustains our cyber-reality mirror the interdependence of the Internet, each node, each module, each chip carry us faithfully into contact with the totality of the entire World Wide Web. May each monitor and tube reflect accurately, reliably, without bias, the data that can become information, the information that can become knowledge, the knowledge that with grace and compassion can become wisdom.
>
> May we stay mindful, as we use our electronic shovels and digital chisels, that the tools are means to an end, that wisdom and compassion are the ends of those means. May our virtual servants clarify our human values and enhance our basic human kindness instead of leading us to serve the technology that too often is designed to serve marketing, marketing that is in turn the servant of greed and the bottom line.

In this way may we make each keystroke a blessing, each printout a prayer, each slideshow a sacrament for the earth and sky.

Monasticism offers a systematic solution to a current crisis of "human values in the hi-tech world." Monastic rules contain a perspective based on virtue and human values. This traditional and consistent point of view provides a useful benchmark from which to review appropriate and inappropriate uses of technology. It is too often the case now that if we can make a tool or a weapon, we will do so without reference to human values. There is no doubt that human society's mores and behavior follow our technological advances. Television, cell phones, computers, e-mail, the World Wide Web, even specific software such as Microsoft Word and what are called massively multiplayer computer games compel us to adapt our behavior to suit the program's needs. Psychiatrists and public health professionals are publishing warnings that the excessive use of computers, leading to addictive behavior, is already out of control. These findings hold true only for developed nations where computer use is widespread. It is also important to acknowledge that between developed and developing countries there are great disparities in opportunity to access the Internet and the information and educational/business opportunities tied to this access. Suppose the power grid went down suddenly, and nobody had privileged access to the hi-tech tools that we have come to rely on? Where would society turn to recall our traditional mores and patterns of virtuous conduct?

Internet addiction in Australia among youth has already reached 30 percent, according to a study from 2007. Korea has an even higher percentage. In the United States, interaction between fathers and children is less than thirty minutes per day. Compare that to the average of 420 minutes that children spend each day with the Internet, television, cell phones, game consoles, and MP3 players.

Monasticism's rootedness in scripture, its emphasis on virtue, compassion, ethical integrity, and service to spiritual values can provide a model for reshaping our priorities as a society. In this regard, the vision of interdependence embedded in the *Pratimoksha* is very helpful in analyzing our relationship with technology. Monasticism offers a potential solution to the crisis of preserving human values in the hi-tech world. Monasteries provide a laboratory for judging appropriate uses of technology. Why? Because embedded in our rule is a time-tested lifestyle that prioritizes spirituality and preserves traditional human values. Monastic rules do not celebrate greed but instead praise sufficiency, simplicity, contentment, gratitude, harmless relationships with all living beings, and interdependence with the natural world.

That we are knit into the fabric of living beings means that monks can advocate and exemplify the ongoing use of embedded ethics, of ancient and sustained wisdom tools—τέχνη (*technē*): tools we make; technology: what people do with their tools. We can identify, hold high, and demonstrate the use of the tools of compassion, wisdom, virtue, kindness, patience, contentment, and selflessness. Because we give priority to these virtues we can authentically say, "No, we don't have to use this new product just because we made it. And we don't have to make it and market this new tool or weapon, simply because we can." We do not have to buy it just because the marketplace tells us it's cool or new. I am suggesting that our monastic rules propose questions that society at large too rarely asks: Is it appropriate technology? What is the standard by which to judge whether or not to make, market, distribute, and use these tools?

Besides helping modern people ask important questions for the future of our planet, monastic rule-based practices can model spiritually awakened, connected lives. Before they eat, monks in the Theravada tradition say,

> Wisely reflecting, I use alms-food not for fun, not for pleasure, not for fattening, not for beautification, but only for mainte-

nance, and nourishment of the body, for keeping it healthy, for helping with the Holy Life, thinking thus: I will allay hunger, without over-eating, so that I can continue to live blamelessly and at ease.

The Mahayana version of this meal blessing, known as the "Five Contemplations," says:

> This offering of the faithful is the fruit of work and care;
> I reflect upon my conduct, "Have I truly earned my share?"
> Of the poisons in the mind the most destructive one is
>   greed;
> As a medicine cures illness, I take only what I need
> To sustain my cultivation, and to realize the Way:
> So we contemplate with gratitude on this offering today.

This example is part of the daily liturgical practices of monks. Liturgy contains skillful ways of celebrating connections with the environment throughout the day. Every day we make our most intimate contact with the environment through our tongue. We physically embody the planet by taking in food through our mouths, food that sustains our lives. By reciting meal blessings we stay cognizant of the reality that we are mendicants and that the food we eat comes to us not through our own work but through the efforts and sacrifice of others. Others' work sustains our very lives. So we reflect on Five Contemplations as we eat: (1) What did I do to earn the food? (2) Did I do anything meritorious to repay the kindness of this offering? (3) I prefer to eat without stirring up greed. We reflect on the fact that the (4) food is medicine that keeps me from the illness of malnutrition. (5) Ultimately we eat to wake up, to help with the Holy Life, to become more wise and compassionate.

These five daily contemplations remind us to be grateful for the offering of food. Blessings such as these at mealtime are practices that

Catholics and Buddhists alike have shared since ancient times. People who live by a monastic rule, who value the invisible and the virtuous, and who keep the old stories alive, can teach us all how to stay neat, that is, how to live skillfully and blamelessly on the earth. Monks can have an important role to play. As the economy depresses and people are forced to make do with less, we can offer them the gift of our monastic practices and the wisdom they contain.

The Rule of Benedict

Sr. Judith Sutera, OSB

If asked to identify the specific teaching of St. Benedict on the environment, most of his followers would be hard pressed to come up with chapter and verse. Benedict never mentions a specific love for nature or a concern for ecology, nor does he acknowledge the relationship between the monastic community and nature.

Yet there must be something inherently healthy in a way of life that has been praised for centuries for its ability to live simply and in harmony with nature. Certainly this has not been the case in all times and places, but, by and large, the good reputation has been there.

If the key is not in his words, his instructions, one might have to look at the Benedictine and conclude that there is some underlying spirit that causes people to act the way they do. First of all, Benedict is not the founder of the monastic tradition in the West. He does not come at the beginning of an innovative period, but at the end of one, as synthesizer and purifier of the tradition. The impulse that first brought Christians to form communities was wrought by the transition from the ideal of the early church and the realities of life under persecution. The early church held up the ideal of holding all things in common and of being above the world's desires for wealth and domination. Indeed, in an environment where being Christian could result in a loss of all one's economic and personal assets, the renunciation was part of a necessary mind-set to accept such a risky faith.

Beyond this kind of practical embrace of simplicity, however, was another primary ideal that moved the first monastics in the desert. Central to their faith was the teaching of Jesus that "the kingdom is here; the kingdom is now." They believed in the eschatological nature of life— that everything should move toward the fulfillment of the kingdom. Paul identified Jesus as the new Adam, the one who had opened the gates of paradise and would restore natural goodness and balance.

These people concluded that, if the kingdom is here and now, then someone ought to be acting like it. What would that life be like, and how—by beginning to model it—can we bring it closer to fulfillment? The catchphrase today is "What would Jesus do?" Perhaps monasticism is founded on the question "Would this happen in Eden?" It is no accident that so many of the desert stories are about the monastics' relationships with animals, the earth providing miraculously for their needs, and the development of communities that were of one heart. It was to be the place where the ideal relationship of all creation began to live again. The desert was to become the flowing garden of primeval holiness.

Benedict, however, does not use any parchment theologizing about this. He simply assumes the premise that a harmonious community of people, committed to living a life that is accountable and holy, will strive to do the right thing. He merely describes in his Rule how those people live and function. Right thinking will evoke right practice and right practice will lead to right thinking.

The foundation of their practice is that they are to live in "the school of the Lord's service." On the most practical of levels, the Benedictine is committed to stability, professes stability. This place and this people will be *my* place and *my* people for my entire life. Stability requires environmental responsibility, because I cannot poison my own well. A farmer does not take everything from the land and then just buy another farm and move. A family may not exhaust all of its resources and expect more to fall from the sky. A neighborhood cannot dump its waste in its own streets and not suffer ill effects of body and spirit.

A monastery that follows the Rule of Benedict is a tangible place and the monastic is a person of a place.

It is no wonder, then, that in past centuries Benedictines, especially Cistercians, contributed so much to the technology and engineering needed for land and water conservation. Benedict does lay the foundation for this in his comment in chapter 66:6, "The monastery should, if possible, be so constructed that within it all necessities . . . are contained." His are practical concerns. He also notes in chapter 55:7 that for other items, such as clothing, the community should "use what is available in the vicinity at a reasonable cost." It is a simple philosophy: How can I provide for my needs in the most effective and nonintrusive way so that my impact on the world in which I live is positive?

Needless to say, modern life has taken us further and further from these goals as we become more and more dependent on others for our energy sources, our food, our material resources. We are trapped in many ways in the modern world's systems, struggling mightily (or sometimes not even motivated to struggle) to reduce our carbon footprint, eat local foods, get off the grid, reduce our waste, and on and on.

The good news, though, is that we are consciously grappling with the issues. Something in our deepest sense of Benedict's teaching is still tugging at our consciousness. Where is it? What is it? I would like to submit one possibility—one that, when I first discovered it some years ago, seemed amazingly obvious once it became conscious. It is in the one place where Benedict does address the relationship of the monastic with all of creation—his chapters on material goods, chapters 31 to 34.

Again, most of what is there is purely practical. The bulk of these chapters deals with very mundane, basic ways in which the goods are distributed and how one relates to them. There is little that is overtly philosophical about the ecology and spirituality of this use and distribution, but it is repeatedly inferred. It is the way in which the person sees him- or herself *in relationship* to the objects that is the focus.

If you were to press the contemporary Benedictine to point to some text in the Rule that indicates that Benedict was ecologically conscious, he or she would most likely go to the tenth verse of chapter 31, where Benedict directs that all things "are to be treated as vessels of the altar." In fact, one cannot get a better and more complete piece of advice than that. I would like, however, to go deeper into his teaching and suggest that it is in the layers of it that one finds an even more profound truth than the already challenging and inspiring literal meaning.

First of all, many monastics forget that the admonition about the vessels of the altar was not originally directed to each individual but to one individual, the cellarer. This person is the true steward of the goods of the monastery; everyone else is to act in obedience to and to follow his or her example. By this person's faithfulness, it can be suggested, the others in the community would be inspired. If they dared to show any less reverence and responsibility in light of the cellarer's generosity and trust, they would certainly be embarrassed and accountable. Good example is usually a more effective means of improving behavior than preaching or punishing.

As anyone who has ever shared any object with another human being, the care of the common is extremely important and a source of either discord or harmony. Benedict provides a whole list of qualities the cellarer is to have. These qualities are essentially the same as those for the abbot and are taken almost verbatim from Paul's list of attributes required of one who is to be appointed a bishop (1 Tim. 3:1–7). The cellarer, then, is an "abbot over things." By extension, then, each person is to give and receive in the same spirit. By extension, also, the person is receiving from one who takes the place of Christ, and thus from Christ.

Whatever is given to be used by the community members is to be given not randomly but as needed. Those who need less should consume less. Those who need more should receive it in humility and recognize that their weakness is being accommodated. This turns the world's notion of consumption upside down. We live in a world that preaches consumption for consumption's sake. If you *can* have it, then you *should* have it. If you can't afford it, you should get it anyway and delay the consequences with credit. If you have more, it is a mark of success, strength, and even happiness. A current TV commercial features a man clutching a credit card and entering an electronics store to get a new television. He moves, enchanted, past walls covered with TVs the size of windows, to those the size of doors, to those the size of double-wide garages. The Greek chorus behind him sings repeatedly, "I want it all, I want it all, I want it all, AND I WANT IT NOW." Has this perhaps become the national anthem?

By contrast, the monastic would move in the opposite direction. Is a smaller one adequate? Do I need it or just want it? Can it wait until later? An "embarrassment of riches" is just that; what a pity that this one is so insecure as to seem to need so much. Benedict does not say that no one should accept additional resources when they are genuinely needed. This, however, is a humble recognition that my health or age or other infirmity causes others to care for me lovingly as is necessary and right.

Benedict is no fan of abject poverty or deprivation for the sake of suffering. He makes clear that each is to have all the essentials for life, if these are available. This is so that people can be freed to concentrate on the important matters of the contemplative life. There is to be mutual trust. If everything one really needs is there, there is no need to hoard or covet or compare or worry. Thus, once again, the "abbot takes the place of Christ in the monastery." I learn, and act out in my interactions, that I can count on a kindly and personal God to make sure that I will not want for the essentials. I get them, however, in humility and through the generous sharing of a communal life. All the members provide for all the members as each is able.

In the monastery, says Benedict, individuals should receive not only according to their need but also according to their ability to use things responsibly. The cellarer issues things to those "in whose manner of life he has confidence" (32:1). Things are given, used, given back. This is the essence of communal life. If we develop the ability to see the whole world as a community, then this is the cycle that is to motivate all life and all use of resources.

As if this were not a powerful enough image, I would like to take it one step further. Probably the most profound and surprising bit of theological insight occurs when one begins to notice that this chapter on the goods of the monastery is reminiscent of another passage in the Rule. Some years ago, I published an article in which I laid out in parallel columns two pieces of the Rule. Their similarities were unmistakable.

Chapter 32: The Tools and Goods of the Monastery

1. The goods of the monastery, that is, its tools, clothing or anything else, should be entrusted to brothers whom the abbot appoints and in whose manner of life he has confidence.

2. He will, as he sees fit, issue to them the various articles to be cared for and collected after use.

3. The abbot will maintain a list of these, so that when the brothers succeed one another in their assigned tasks, he may be aware of what he hands out and what he receives back.

4. Whoever fails to keep the things belonging to the monastery clean or treats them carelessly should be reproved.

5. If he does not amend, let him be subjected to the discipline of the rule.

Chapter 4: The Tools for Good Works

5. These, then, are the tools of the spiritual craft.

(following verses list commandments, works of mercy, and other practices for a holy life)

76. When we have used them without ceasing day and night and have returned them on judgment day, our wages will be the reward the Lord has promised.

78. The workshop where we are to toil faithfully at all these tasks is the enclosure of the monastery and stability in the community.

The cosmic wholeness of St. Benedict's sense of the world is summed up in these simple paragraphs. There is no such thing as a small act or a meaningless act in life if one lives in mindfulness. Everything points to a total and universal truth—that all creation is united in the movement toward its ultimate unity and harmony. Every time I pick up a broom or a hammer, every time I run water or turn on an appliance, I am acting out my understanding of the final judgment: that all that I have has been given as gift and I must return it both positively maintained and positively used.

As if this were not a clear enough mandate, I would like to return to that lovely line about the vessels of the altar and add even one more layer. This line is not original to Benedict. It is another one of his pervasive scriptural citations, coming from an obscure line of the prophet Zechariah, who decrees that "the pots ... shall be as the libation bowls before the altar. And every pot in Jerusalem and in Judah shall be holy to the lord of hosts" (14:20–21). The prophet was making one of the "on that day" prophecies. When the day of the Lord comes, and Jerusalem is restored, everything will be a vessel of the altar. Thus Benedict evokes the eschatological image: everything has become sacred in the already/not-yet kingdom, the new Jerusalem/new Eden that the monastery is to symbolize. Every person is a sanctified minister of God, ennobled and empowered to share in the divine mysteries and the divine ministry.

If once every thousand times we used a tool or a natural resource, we would realize the totality of this truth, we would be transformed. If by our example, we could bring others to this awareness, they too might be transformed. Yet to develop such mindfulness is always a challenge. Once again, we return to the notion of thinking shaping practice and practice shaping thinking.

We have to continue to ask ourselves hard questions in a time of great complexity. It is no longer reasonable to assume that everything we need will be produced and contained in the monastery, but how do we at least keep reminding ourselves about our dependencies? How do we develop awareness of where things come from and how they are produced? How committed are we to live simply? How much can we adjust our expectations . . . and do we even want to? If we cannot do everything, do we at least attempt to do something? If we do have bountiful resources, how do we preserve them, reverence them, share them, steward them?

The central question remains, "If the kingdom is here and the kingdom is now, who will act like it? Would this happen in Eden?" If people cannot look to those who are supposed to be connected to the spiritual world, those who are supposed to understand the unity of all creation, to whom can they look? We don't have to be perfect, but we have to be trying.

In the *Life of St. Benedict,* St. Gregory tells us that shortly before he died Benedict saw the whole world gathered up before his eyes in what appeared to be a single ray of light. "All creation," Gregory explains, "is bound to appear small to a soul that sees the creator." What he means is not that contemplation raises one to such heights that the entire world is insignificant; rather, with true perspective, the one who stands in the divine presence is able to see the entire world as a single entity, a single responsibility. The contemplative human, inside or outside the monastery, is able to see all acts in every single act, and all life in a single light.

IV

Monasticism and the
Consumer Society

The Monastic Instinct to Revere, to Conserve, to Be Content with Little, and to Share

Rev. Eko Little

In 1418 a competition was announced in the city of Florence, Italy, for the design and building of the dome of the new cathedral of Santa Maria del Fiore. The participants had six weeks to build models, draw designs, and make suggestions on how to vault the largest cathedral dome ever built. Sponsoring the competition was the *Opera del Duomo*, the office of works in charge of building the cathedral, which was begun in 1296. With a handsome commission and plenty of prestige at stake to attract the most talented designers of the time, more than a dozen models were submitted for consideration. But the most daring and unorthodox model did not come from a famous architect, builder, or mason; instead, it was the brainchild of jeweler and clockmaker Filippo Brunelleschi.[1]

Brunelleschi's model of the dome spanned six feet and was twelve feet high. It needed forty-nine cartloads of quicklime to harden the mortar, which held five thousand bricks together. It was big enough for a person to walk inside and inspect its construction. Brunelleschi's model omitted the wooden framing usually required to build any kind of a dome, and this radical departure completely distinguished his design from anyone else's. So different was his approach that the *Opera*'s wardens were completely baffled about how he was going to build it. Filippo's design plans were a complete mystery. He was very secretive; he did not discuss his plans, he submitted no drawings, and he always worked alone, with only one or two other trusted assistants to help him. Finally, when the cathedral wardens demanded to know how he would build the actual dome, Filippo refused to tell them. The wardens called him "an ass and a babbler," and they tossed him bodily out of one meeting during a spirited conversation about the dome's construction. Finally, Filippo proposed to the group of wardens that whoever among the competitors could make an egg stand on end on a flat piece of marble should be given the commission. When all the other contestants failed the test, Filippo simply tapped the egg on its narrow bottom and stood it upright. The other competitors protested that they could have done the same had they known the method, and Filippo pointed out that likewise they would all know how to vault the dome if they knew his plans. The *Opera del Duomo* grudgingly accepted Filippo's model for the new dome; and, after many difficulties, trials, and tribulations, Filippo Brunelleschi completed the dome of Santa Maria del Fiore in 1436. Pope Eugenius IV consecrated the cathedral one month later, sixteen years and two weeks after construction had begun.

Filippo Brunelleschi knew how to make an egg stand on its end. The humble egg is an unremarkable object familiar to everyone. Millions of pounds of eggshells are thrown away each day without much thought given to the proportion and design of that elegant oval. But how many people know how to make an egg stand upright? An egg standing on end is the perfect metaphor for the monastic life. The very ordinary egg, which no one thinks twice about, when handled by someone with special wisdom, who recognizes its shape and all that its shape is capable of, can be made to do something quite remarkable. In the same way, the wisdom of a monastic, which comes from his/her vows and religious practice, enables the monastic to do something that very few people know how to do: find true happiness and contentment within themselves. That happiness comes not from prestige, fame, gain, accomplishment, wealth, or property, but from the intentional cultivation of reverence, renunciation, gratitude, and generosity. These monastic instincts are the egg standing on end.

Although Filippo Brunelleschi had built his model of the dome of Santa Maria, he had not yet worked out the details of how he would build the actual dome itself. He did not fully know how he was going to do it, but he believed that he could, and his ingenious construction methods were all developed over the course of the cathedral's construction. Filippo had faith in his ability to begin construction of the dome and to complete it successfully. A monastic cultivates religious faith to lead a life of reverence, renunciation, gratitude, and generosity. However, learning the practical cultivation of these virtues is something that gets worked out as we go along. We have to cultivate the faith needed to meet and overcome the obstacles, both internal and external, that are inevitable in the religious life. Even though we do not know how to do it when we start, we cannot allow that to prevent us from going ahead. Monastic virtues are both created and discovered in the creative work of living the monastic life. We learn how to do it by doing it. Our monastic lives are composed of the very virtues that can help to save the world in the midst of the modern environmental crisis, which we all must face. With faith and determination, these virtues can be cultivated and practiced by anyone not just monastics. Everyone can learn how to stand an egg on end.

The founder of the Soto Zen tradition in Japan, Eihei Dogen (1200–1252 CE), was advised by his Chinese master to find a place "deep in the mountains, away from the world" where he might practice the Way of the Buddhas. Nowadays, Dogen is regarded as a kind of Buddhist Thoreau, embraced by Buddhists and non-Buddhists alike as an environmental prophet many centuries ahead of his time. We are likely to see his name linked more and more with environmental issues, and his voluminous writings will undoubtedly be quoted many times over. Dogen's writings and teachings deserve to be included and studied in this modern context.

As with many prophets, Dogen's teachings are often misunderstood, his words often misquoted, and his meaning somewhat distorted. Because his works are rich in natural imagery, he is popularly thought of as a nature mystic, a kind of Buddhist St. Francis. Indeed, it is easy to think of him this way, especially since one of his more famous discourses is entitled "The Mountains and Rivers Sutra." But Dogen was not an environmental prophet; instead, he was a revolutionary religious thinker and monastic. He saw the relationship between the sentient and nonsentient world, between the human world and the natural, as a radical religious fusion. Once we understand his deep and far-reaching religious vision, Dogen becomes a true luminary of the monastic view of the environment as well as a real prophet of a sacred and sustainable environmental culture.

One of the themes of our encounter is the monastic instinct to revere. Dogen's vision of the Eternal, which he called Buddha Nature, can be described as reverential realization. Dogen believed that *everything* is Buddha Nature. Buddha Nature is the essence of Buddhahood that permeates all beings. Everyone is endowed with Buddha Nature, and each and every one of us can fully realize Buddha Nature through our religious practice. To Dogen, however, it was insufficient to say that all beings are endowed with Buddha Nature or have Buddha Nature: everyone *is* Buddha Nature. And not just every *one*—every *thing* is Buddha Nature, too. Every one and every thing, be it sentient or insentient, is Buddha Nature. The only way, then, to practice the Buddha Nature of every thing and every one is to treat everyone and everything as Buddha Nature. To Dogen, everyone and everything is literally the living body of the Buddha.

In Dogen's view, both human beings and the physical world are the living expression of the life of the Buddha. *Everything* is the object of veneration of the living essence of Buddha Nature. When this vision is applied to the environment, the implication for environmental consciousness is staggering. Nothing is mundane; everything becomes sacred. That which is sacred must be revered, protected, preserved, and maintained. Reverence is not only an attitude of mind; there must also be a physical expression of that reverential attitude. One treats everything as if it were—because it is—the living tissue of Buddhahood. If you think this through, this view means saving the entire world and everything that is in it through the way we live, because the way we live is our realization of religious practice, and that practice itself is the vehicle of reverence. Dogen's view of the indivisibility of Buddha Nature is a religious mandate for environmental stewardship as well as for the enlightenment of human society. It is a mandate not only given for the sake of helping living beings but given for the sake of helping everything. It is for the sake of everything and everyone that one venerates, reveres, cherishes, and takes care of the world.

Everything is Buddha Nature, and everything is equal in that Buddha Nature. The grasses and the trees, the mountains and the rivers, says Dogen, proclaim the Buddha's teaching just as eloquently, just as equally, as any human being does. There is no boundary between the sentient and the insentient; the insentient communicate their sacred equality just as eloquently as the sentient. Creatures and things express their life each in their own way, and they communicate that life in ways that nowadays we can actually observe through our senses, understand intellectually, and even measure scientifically. This is the essence of Dogen's religious vision: everything (and everyone) is Buddha Nature. Therefore, we must treat it as such and care for it with reverence (love), renunciation (nongreed), gratitude, and generosity.

The deep realization that Buddha Nature is everything and everything is Buddha Nature permeates the entirety of Dogen's thought and teaching. However, he was not just a philosopher. First and foremost, Dogen was a monastic as well as the founding abbot of a community of monks. He applied his vision practically to encompass and govern all the aspects of monastic life, from the most sublime down to

the most earthy. This man who wrote the "Mountains and Rivers" discourse also gave his monks clear instructions on how to use little clay
balls to clean themselves after defecating and how to use the tooth-
brush, accompanied with prayers taken from the scriptures to remind
them of what they were doing and why. His writings are full of these
practical methods, each accompanied with exhortations to focus the
mind on contemplation and spiritual realization.

For instance, since everything is Buddha Nature, nothing is to be
wasted, especially food. In his work called the *Tenzokyokan,* "Instructions to the Chief Cook," Dogen gives clear guidance on how the
monastery food (in this case, rice and water) is to be prepared and
cared for. He says,

> Once the food has been prepared it must be cared for in the
> same way as we care for our own eyesight; the common prop-
> erty of the temple must be accorded the same care as that
> accorded to our own eyes. This food must be dealt with as if
> it were for the royal table; exactly the same care must be given
> to all food, whether raw or cooked.[2]

He directed that the water in which the daily rice was washed was to
be strained to make sure that even a grain of rice did not escape.

> The water with which the rice is washed must not idly be
> thrown away; in the old days a straining bag was used for the
> purpose of ensuring that no rice was ever left in the water . . . .
> Every grain of rice must be washed carefully . . . by the Chief
> Cook personally; he must never leave until the washing is over
> and he must, on no account, cast away even a single grain . . . .[3]

Dogen did not just focus on food; the kitchen pots were seen as part
of Buddha Nature and were to be cared for with the same spirit of
devotion: ". . . the pot in which the rice is cooked must be thought of as

our own heads; the water in which the rice is washed must be thought of as our own life."[4]

In our tradition, "The Instructions to the Chief Cook" is a model for the way all the monastery seniors should carry out their duties, including the abbot. The monastery cook must be able to see the Buddha Nature in everything; he or she must be content with the quality of food offered to and purchased for the monastery and do his or her best to prepare the food that is to be cooked for that day. Above all, he/she must be able to see and show the Buddha Nature within it. Dogen says,

> The Chief Cook must not eye the food superficially or with a discriminatory [judgmental] mind; his spirit must be so free that the Buddha Land appears within a blade of grass, whenever he and others behold it, and he must be capable of giving a great sermon even on the very heart of a particle of dust. He must not be contemptuous when making poor quality soup, nor should he be overjoyed when he makes it with milk; if he is unattached to the last, he will not hate the first. There must be no laziness in him, however unappetizing the food may be; should the food he beholds be of good quality his training must become all the deeper so that he might avoid attachment thereto. His speech in the presence of all men must be the same, unchanging in mode for, should he change it, he is not a true seeker after Buddhahood. He must be polite in all he does and strenuous in perfecting his efforts at cooking, for these actions will lead him in the path of purity and care once trodden by the excellent monks of old: I myself long to be thus.[5]

He also says,

> It is absolutely essential that the pure actions of the Chief Cook shall come forth from his realization of unity with all

things and beings; having no prejudices himself, he must be able to see into the minds and hearts of others . . . . from only a stalk of cabbage, he seems to produce a sixteen-foot-long body of the Buddha.[6]

Dogen taught that the chief cook must cultivate three fundamental virtues: gratitude, love, and generosity. The monastic cook must cultivate gratitude and express that gratitude in the way that he or she serves the monastic community. Dogen says,

> How lucky we are. How blessed is this body: for all eternity there will be no greater opportunity than that offered to us now; its merit is undefileable. When we serve our fellow monks purely, hundreds and thousands of lives are enfolded in one single day's or hour's work, which will bear fruit for many lives to come; to grasp Truth thus is clearly to express gratitude.[7]

Reverence for Buddha Nature, which we Buddhists would express as devotion to the Three Treasures of Buddha, Dharma, and Sangha, is the mind of love. Dogen explains that the cook must love the materials of his work in the same way that he loves the Three Treasures, and likens that love to the way parents love their children. Think of this kind of love in terms of cherishing our entire world, with the beings and things that exist within it. Dogen writes,

> The mind of our parents expresses love and we must love the Three Treasures in the same way as our parents love us. However poor a person may be it is frequently possible to see the love he expresses towards his children; who is capable of understanding the extent of his loving mind other than he himself? All men, whether rich or poor, long for their children to grow strong and big, protecting them with unsparing

devotion against inclement weather; this is the greatest of all sincerity; no one who does not possess this mind can understand it. A Chief Cook must love water and rice in the same way that parents love their children; the Buddha gave us forty-five years of his life because he wanted to teach us parental love by his example . . . .[8]

Here is a monastic model of love that cherishes Buddha Nature in all things, while devoting itself selflessly in service to the monastic community as it protects the resources of the community. Here is an example of a heart and mind that are at one with the spiritual source, and that express that spiritual unity by selflessly loving the things of the earth and the activity of those things in the same way that parents love their children. This mind of love based on reverence is the foundation for an ultraresponsible stewardship of the earth and all the things contained within it.

Charity—sharing, generosity—is the foremost Buddhist virtue; all Buddhist morality begins with charity, which we call *dana*. It is charity that opens the heart and enables us to care for something other than ourselves. Dogen says,

[T]he offering of only one coin or blade of grass can cause the arising of good, for the Teaching itself is the True Treasure and the True Treasure is the very teaching; we must never desire any reward and we must always share everything we have with others. It is an act of charity to build a ferry or a bridge and all forms of industry are charity if they benefit others.[9]

"If they benefit others," he says. But what if others are harmed by industry? What if industry harms the resources of life for all beings by fouling the water, polluting the air, and unnaturally accelerating the warming of the planet? If this kind of industry harms others, then there appears a moral obligation to change our industrial practices in order that they will help, not harm, the delicate web of life. This kind of action is consistent with the spirit of Right Livelihood, one of our most fundamental teachings. And, it has to be done in a spirit of loving-kindness, compassion, charity, tenderness, benevolence, and sympathy. Here is a real project for human beings.

This is only a shadow of Dogen's teachings, but it gives you a good sense of how the monastic life becomes a template for an environmental renaissance. In Buddhism, there is more than enough teaching to serve as a wholesome foundation for environmental awareness and education, and as a support for compassionate, vigorous, and decisive action.

In our monastery, we are trying to adopt available technology for cleaner and more efficient energy. We're vegetarians. We have a vigorous recycling program. We try to conserve as much as possible, and we try not to waste and to make our resources stretch as far as we can. We are careful not to buy more than we need and to keep our needs simple. We try to purchase green products, and we have a long-term plan for greening our monastery. We live on donations, so the limitations are obvious. But, we are still trying to do our part, and we are continually looking for better ways to reduce our environmental impact. We are "active-contemplatives," and in our teaching we are trying to emphasize the qualities of monastic life and general Buddhist practice that can help people cultivate the faith and determination to solve the difficult environmental issues of our day. As all of you are aware, the grave problems that we humans experience, including our environmental challenges, are fundamentally spiritual problems.

I personally feel that the environmental situation is very grave, and I am trying to remain positive. We can already see the signs that the beings of our world in this and coming generations already experience the hard consequences of our lack of wise stewardship and will continue to do so. There will doubtless be many difficult and painful choices to be made in order to affect and reverse the environmental damage that has already been done. In dealing with those problems, the virtues of the monastic life become an invaluable resource and actually contain the blueprint for success: reverence, renunciation, noble poverty, generosity, celibacy, compassion, conservation, selfless service, education, faith, morality, kindness. . . . The list goes on and on. In coming years, people may well have to learn to live more like monastics, learning to be content with less, as conditions force us all to elevate our vision in order to do what will be necessary to sustain the natural conditions for life on our earth.

My prayer is that we monastics can have a positive influence, that we can be like the egg standing on end. Through our monastic lives and vows, we can take something very ordinary and transform it into something extraordinary. We can show people by example how to be happy and fulfilled without having to have a lot of stuff. We can help others by inspiring them to cultivate a life of virtue that seeks to help all beings as it cherishes the world and all the marvels contained within it. These virtues are the pathway to human happiness and, eventually, to enlightenment itself. May we all realize it together; may all beings be happy; may all be free from suffering.

Christian Monasticism and Simplicity of Life

Fr. Charles Cummings, OCSO

In a consumer society, those who follow the monastic way are marching out of step because they can be content with a simple lifestyle. Allow me to begin with true confessions. For many years, my life as a monk was simple. It was a simple round of chanting, manual labor, periods of reading and prayer, with no more personal belongings than I could put into my desk drawers and a couple of clothes lockers. I cannot pinpoint exactly when I began to lose simplicity in my life, but I no longer have it now. What I have now is a whirlwind of multiplicity and complexity, a race against the calendar and the clock. I hate to blame everything on my computer, but as I look back, I remember a time in the mid-80s when I acquired my first computer and made the transition from typewriter to this new technology that was supposed to simplify my correspondence, creative writing, and research. But it has turned out to be a technology still prone to freeze-ups and breakdowns, loss of data, and a resulting increase of work. Next came Internet and e-mail, intended further to simplify my duties. Instead, I began to spin faster and faster, not in the prayerful way of the whirling dervishes but with the mindlessness of a toy top going nowhere fast. Now, if it is not too late, I want to get off this merry-go-round and get back to the simple life, back to center, before I spin totally out of control, like an unguided monastic missile on the way to outer space. Where is the wisdom that will point me to simplicity of life?

One place is the Wisdom literature of the Hebrew Scriptures, where we find this thought in Ecclesiastes: "This is all that I have learned: God made us plain and simple, but we have made ourselves very complicated" (Eccl. 7:29; Good News Translation). King David was in some respects a complicated man, but his devotion to Yahweh was simple, even childlike. After piling up mountains of precious metals and costly building materials for the temple, he offered it all to Yahweh in a grand gesture: "I know, my God, that you put hearts to the test and love simplicity. Wherefore I also in the simplicity of my heart have joyfully offered all these things" (1 Chr. 29:17; Douay-Rheims).

Jesus seems to have equated simplicity of heart with a quality of childlike trust in God's care. On one occasion, "He called a child over, placed it in their midst, and said, 'Amen, I say to you, unless you turn and become like children, you will not enter the kingdom of heaven'" (Matt. 8:2–3; NAB as also in subsequent citations). Jesus himself in his public ministry lived in radical simplicity as an itinerant preacher, freely receiving and freely giving: "Foxes have dens and birds of the sky have nests, but the Son of Man has nowhere to rest his head" (Luke 9:58). He cautioned against crass materialism to the neglect of the spirit: "Do not store up for yourselves treasures on earth, where moth and decay destroy, and thieves break in and steal. But store up treasures in heaven, where neither moth nor decay destroys, nor thieves break in and steal" (Matt. 6:19–20). He told the parable of the rich man who tore down his barns and built larger ones to hold all his goods but that night had to face his eternal judgment. "Thus will it be for the one who stores up treasure for himself but is not rich in what matters to God" (Luke 12:21).[1]

What do I mean by simplicity of life? Simplicity as I understand it has two levels: material and spiritual. On the material level, a simple life means a life that is uncluttered, free of the superfluous, content with the necessities.[2] St. Paul reminds Timothy: "We brought nothing into the world, just as we shall not be able to take anything out of it.

If we have food and clothing, we shall be content with that" (1 Tim. 6:7–8). Such a list prompts us to ask how much is really enough. I myself would prefer to add at least a couple of items to Paul's short list: food, clothing, a roof that does not leak, and a computer.

On the spiritual level, a simple life suggests simplicity of heart, a heart that is centered on the one thing necessary (Luke 10:42), that is, the love of God or the kingdom of God. On this level, simplicity is a rich and full experience, a life that is integrated, not fragmented but unified in the sense of the Greek *monos*, which is the root of the word *monk*. To reach this level of interior simplification usually takes a conscious ascetic effort in order to detach oneself from all distracting desires.[3]

Poet T. S. Eliot in *Four Quartets* may be speaking of material and spiritual simplicity at the same time when he describes "A condition of complete simplicity (Costing not less than everything)" ("Little Gidding V"). Does he really mean "everything"? Isn't that going to an extreme? Or does simplicity beckon us to an extreme because there is something godlike about it? The closer we draw to God, the simpler we become. St. Teresa of Avila says "God alone suffices" ("*solo Dios basta*"). God alone. Catholic scholastic theology talks of God as a reality not only without component parts but without any composition whatsoever, not even essence and existence, for the essence of God is God's own existence (Thomas Aquinas, *Summa Theologiae*, PP 3). Therefore the lovely ballad in Leonard Bernstein's *Mass* is right on the mark with the words:

> Sing God a simple song: *Lauda, Laude.*
> Make it up as you go along: *Lauda, Laude.*
> Sing like you like to sing.
> God loves all simple things.
> For God is the simplest of all.

Christian monastic tradition fosters a life of simplicity by surrounding the monk with some degree of silence, enclosure, natural beauty, a predictable schedule, daily and seasonal rhythms, and limited contact with society outside the monastery. In such conditions, a monk's mind and heart can drop their defenses and open up to all that is true and good, open up to the seed of God's word in scripture. That is simplicity as openness. The monk can gather all of himself/herself into one and center his/her heart on the love of God. That is simplicity as single-minded single heartedness.

Monks accustomed to a simple life are secure and comfortable being who they are. They are unpretentious in what they say and how they act, without duplicity or hidden agendas, the same outside and inside. I do not mean they are simpletons in the negative sense, but in a positive way they are grounded in truth, humility, gratitude, and love. They are ready to love with their whole heart, soul, mind, and strength, because their heart is undivided and uncluttered.

Concern for simplicity has led monks to reject the superfluous and to discover that less—not more—of something is often more beautiful and tasteful. I do not wish to get into the controversies about architecture, church furnishings, liturgical music and ceremonies, and religious art that sometimes set black monks (Benedictines) against white monks (Cistercians) in the Middle Ages and later. I think there is room for various expressions of a common ideal. But in this context it may be worth recalling some recent nonmonastic witnesses like British economist Ernst Schumacher (1911–77), who promoted "technology with a human face" in his 1973 book *Small Is Beautiful: Economics as if People Mattered.* Then there is the twentieth-century movement of minimalism in art, music, literature, the performing arts, and especially architecture, as, for example, in the Czech Cistercian abbey Novy Dvur designed by London architect John Pawson, completed in 2004. These are contemporary witnesses to simplicity.

There are other examples—nonmonastic examples—of living simply: groups that are characterized by their simplicity as well as individuals. Without going too far back in history we find communities, often of religious inspiration, that choose to live frugally, close to the land, at a horse-and-buggy pace, cherishing the values of family and community, content with the basics when it comes to food, furnishings, and clothing. In the eighteenth century there was an influx of these groups to the United States. I am thinking of the Amish, the Mennonites, the Shakers. In the mid-twentieth century the Bruderhof immigrated to this country and joined with the Hutterites but since have split from them.

To return to the Shakers for a minute, they had a community called Pleasant Hill, located about seventy miles east of Gethsemani Abbey, which was active for slightly more than a century until 1910, was restored in the 1960s, and is now a National Historic Landmark.[4] One of the most well known and loved Shaker hymns goes as follows:

> 'Tis the gift to be simple,
> 'tis the gift to be free,
> 'tis the gift to come down
> where we ought to be,
> and when we find ourselves in the place just right,
> 'twill be in the valley of love and delight.
> When true simplicity is gained
> to bow and to bend we shan't be ashamed,
> to turn, turn, will be our delight
> till by turning, turning we come round right.[5]

As for individuals, when we learn about or meet someone who has a radically simple lifestyle, we sense their integrity and substance, their dedication to their chosen path. It is enough to invoke the names of some of these people who are better known, apart from Jesus himself:

> St. Francis of Assisi, 1182–1226
> Henry David Thoreau, 1817–62
> St. Bernadette Soubirous, 1844–79

St. Thérèse of Lisieux, 1873–97
Mahatma Gandhi, 1869–1948
Pope John XXIII, 1881–1963
Dorothy Day, 1897–1980
Peace Pilgrim, 1908–81[6]

The simple lifestyle of such people is countercultural, no matter when they lived. If monks today opt for a simpler lifestyle, we too will go counter to the consumer society around us. Our choices will challenge the greed and wastefulness, the pollution and sheer noise that people accept as inevitable parts of life, especially urban life. Consumerism, fed by incessant advertising, is an addiction to buying unnecessary and often impractical new merchandise in order to fill an inner incompleteness. People forget that "Whoever dies with the most toys is still dead." In what ways might we as monks simplify our lives in the interest of being more ecologically sensitive? In answer I propose three "Rs": Reduce consumption, Recycle, and Rely more on one's local community.

1. *Reduce consumption.* The current jargon for reducing one's impact on the environment is to "reduce your carbon footprint." This does not mean taking off your shoes before coming indoors, although that may be a good idea. Our carbon footprint is the amount of carbon dioxide we release into the atmosphere by such activities as driving a car or using electricity generated from coal. Some people try to give up nonessential carbon emissions for Lent. Others buy carbon credits by planting trees that consume CO_2. Vatican City plants trees in Hungary to offset its carbon footprint.

2. *Recycle and repair.* Living in a throwaway culture where goods are engineered to break down or become obsolete in a few years, monks can sometimes mend what tears, can repair what breaks down instead of pitching it, or can be content with using an older, less-convenient model for a little longer. When we do throw something out, we can try to throw it in the proper receptacle for recycling. Some monaster-

ies have various receptacles for paper, glass, aluminum or other metals, compost material, and plastic. Jesus told his disciples, "Gather the fragments left over, so that nothing will be wasted" (John 6:12). You have also heard: "One person's trash is another person's treasure." It is true. To give one example, our obsolete computers, monitors, televisions, and cell phones, discarded at the rate of about three million tons per year in the United States, can be smelted down and the valuable components extracted and reused.[7] Recycling goes with a simple lifestyle because it disciplines the instinct to hoard, the pack-rat syndrome. On the other hand, too much compulsiveness about recycling can also complicate one's life instead of simplifying it.

3. *Rely* on yourself in order to be as self-sustaining as possible. This advice applies to monasteries more than to individual monks. For centuries in the Christian West, monasteries were largely self-sustaining, according to the principle in the Rule of St. Benedict 66.6: "The monastery should, if possible, be so constructed that within it all necessities, such as water, mill and garden are contained, and the various crafts are practiced." In today's interdependent world economy, a monastery might succeed in being partially self-sustaining. Some food needs could be met by a vegetable garden and a greenhouse, and maybe animals. Energy dependence could be reduced by use of solar, wind, or geothermal resources. For example, the Trappists at New Melleray, Iowa, heat and cool their casket factory by an underground geothermal system, and St. Mary Monastery in Rock Island, Illinois, has a geothermal system to cool and heat their monastery from an artificial lake about one acre in area with five miles of piping beneath it. The Trappistines at Mount St. Mary's in Wrentham, Massachusetts, with the help of a grant, are installing a wind turbine that is expected to generate enough electricity to meet all the needs of the monastery.

In today's interconnected world, simplified living is practically an issue of justice, that is, a moral issue. Because of this moral dimension, Pope Benedict on numerous occasions has been a strong spokesman for responsible ecology, and so has the Dalai Lama. How can developed countries or monks in developed countries justify patterns of conspicuous consumption and thoughtless waste when so many human beings live in near destitution in developing countries? "The fruits of the earth were given to feed all," says St. Ambrose.[8] The best motto is "to live simply, that others may simply live."[9]

Because the price of crude oil today is rising, everything that depends on oil in our postindustrial society costs us more—not only transportation, but also plastics, chemicals, and fertilizers, with a ripple effect all down the line. For an oil-dependent economy, a petrocivilization such as the United States, the party is over. Perhaps that will be a good thing for us from the spiritual point of view, a blessing in disguise, for it may provide the incentive we need to move away from consumerism and materialism toward voluntary simplicity of life.[10]

V

Contemporary Environmental Practices in American Monastic Communities

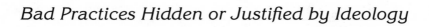

Bad Practices Hidden or Justified by Ideology

Saffron and Green in the Clear Forest Pool

*A Reflection on the Four Noble Truths
and Right Effort*

Ayya Tathaaloka Bhikkhuni

The clear forest pool is a place where we come for reflection and insight, to see not only what is on the surface but what is deep within: saffron, the color of our Buddhist monastic robe; and green, loving care for our environment.

Our Buddhist monastic community is founded on and well endowed with effective practices of honest self-reflection and introspection, an eye for the interrelatedness of conditions that lead to either our harm or welfare, and a heart of great and compassionate caring sensitivity for humanity and all living beings. We seem well equipped for the task we are now called to: identifying the "bad practices," hidden or justified by ideology, that might be present in our American Buddhist monastic communities. If they do exist—and I believe they do—they have neither been readily apparent nor quickly and easily forthcoming. Uncovering them has required a good amount of effort. Still, the task is both a noble and an urgent one. In fact, it is a task called for by the Noble Eightfold Path itself in its definition of Right Effort.

Let us begin with the crucial fourfold practice of Right Effort that appears in the Noble Eightfold Path. By definition, Right Effort is also known as Wise Endeavor and Right Striving, and is what all practicing Buddhists are supposed to apply their energies to, doing so diligently, vigilantly, valiantly, persistently, and energetically. Within the circular wheel illustrating the Noble Eightfold Path, Right Effort is related to Right and Wise Livelihood. Right Livelihood is informed by Right View and then enacted in our intentions, thoughts, words, and deeds. Right Effort is also intimately related to and dependent upon Right Mindfulness and Recollection, Clear Comprehension, and Full Awareness or Presence.

The operative scheme of Right Effort is fourfold. In all cases the monastic (or lay) practitioners are guided by the Buddha to generate desire, make an effort, activate persistence, and uphold and exert their intent for:

1. the nonarising of whatever evil, unskillful qualities have not yet arisen;
2. the reduction and cessation of whatever evil, unskillful qualities have arisen;
3. the arising of skillful qualities that have not yet arisen;
4. the maintenance, nonconfusion, increase, plentitude, development, and culmination of skillful qualities that have already arisen.

Qualities that are "evil" and "unskillful"—in Pali *papa* and *akusala*—are generally defined as those that cause short- or long-term harm, detriment, or suffering to ourselves or to others. These are the "bad practices" for which we are looking. By "others" is meant not only our fellow humans but all forms of life. Qualities that are "skillful"—in Pali *kusala*—are generally defined as those good and wholesome thoughts, words, or actions that lead to short- and long-term well-being, peace, and happiness for ourselves and for others—again, not only for our fellow human beings but for all forms of life.

This is the basic operating framework of Right Effort. It assumes the development of Right View—that is, knowledge relating to cause and effect—in order to come to an understanding of what is evil and what is skillful. It also assumes the development of both mindfulness and clear awareness in relation to context—that is, what will be right, wise, wholesome, and skillful to do in a particular situation.

Given this teaching—the basic foundational doctrine of all schools of Buddhism—we cannot fault the Buddha for what lay and monastic Buddhist, both Western and Eastern, may have done to harm our local and global environment and welfare. I believe the teaching of the Buddha is perfect. It is for us to understand it and put it into action— to *strive* to put into action through right and wise effort.

And yet, despite the fact that Right Effort clearly and skillfully covers the ground of what most all of us would like to do all the time anyway—reduce and eliminate the bad and perpetuate the good—it is perhaps the most widely unknown and most prevalently misunderstood of all of the basic teachings of the Buddha. This is true, at least in America today, both in the public at large as well as within the Buddhist community. We will look more into why I say this below.

In 2004, the U.S. Department of State estimated there were 5.6 million Buddhists in the United States. (The number of Buddhists worldwide is 350 to 500 million.) The number of Christian-Buddhists, Jew-Bu's (Jewish Buddhists), and U-Bu's (Unitarian Universalist Buddhists) is also quite substantial. In addition, the number of Buddhist monastics and monastic communities in the West is slowly but steadily on the rise. We who are Buddhists in America cannot and should not say that we have not participated in, or are not participating in and contributing to, our world's environmental situation. We are not simply passive observers or ineffective participants. Rather, our every thought, word, and act contributes to the well-being or the harming of our environment. Our choices make a difference. We are active and important participants, no matter how passive or inconsequential we imagine our role to be.

In preparation for reflecting on the environmental practices of American Buddhist monasteries I posted the following question on

Insight Forum, an e-network of several thousand Buddhists in the San Francisco Bay Area: Are there bad environmental practices hidden or justified by Buddhist ideology in our American Buddhist monastic communities? The responses I received from members of the forum, as well as others that came from contemplative Western and Eastern Buddhist monastic and lay practitioners and mentors around the world, will complement my own personal thoughts and the Buddha's teaching. This will help us see ourselves in our local context as well as within the greater global context.

The responses to this question have largely fallen into two categories that roughly correspond to the terms "hidden" and "justified by ideology" in the question. Hidden, bad environmental practices were seen by the vast majority of Buddhist respondents as stemming from superficial or incomplete understanding of what the Buddha actually taught. Bad environmental practices justified by ideology were seen by the majority of respondents as being based on partial, questionable, unskillful, or even dubious understanding of the Buddha's teachings taken out of their proper context.

Since the Buddha considered misunderstanding to be at the root of all problems, it is not surprising that misunderstanding should also be at the root of our environmental problems. This misunderstanding, in turn, gives rise to misrepresentations of the Buddha's teachings that can be related to the environmental crisis today. In response to the question before us, the Venerable Ajahn Pasanno, co-abbot of Abhayagiri Forest Monastery and environmental activist within the Thai Buddhist Forest Tradition, said:

> What comes up are the themes of misrepresenting the teachings and intention of the Buddha through such things as equanimity being seen as indifference, relinquishing of desire as an excuse for non-action, karma being interpreted as everybody deserves what they get so why do anything about it, contentment being used as a reason for complacency.

The first and most prevalent misunderstanding that has repeatedly come to light is related to the most fundamental of the Buddha's teachings, the Four Noble Truths. The adult child of a Buddhist parent once told me that since "life is suffering" and since the cause of that suffering is attachment, all that is to be done is to abandon it and let it go. He was ready to give up on life and the world as hopeless and fatally flawed. Since everything was impermanent, the only thing to do was to "blow it off." Such a misunderstanding of the Buddha's teaching on suffering can make people inactive, complacent and apathetic, negative, even depressed, unable to act effectively for their own welfare or that of their society and world.

Let us take a look at the true understanding of the Buddha's teaching concerning disenchantment, renunciation, and release related to the world. It is true that in the Third Noble Truth of the Ending of Suffering the Buddha says:

> This, monks, is the Noble Truth of the Ending of Suffering: the remainderless fading away and stopping, renunciation, relinquishment, release, and letting go of that very craving [that is, craving for sensual pleasure, craving for becoming, and craving for nonbecoming].

The Middle Way stands free and clear of the opposing extremes of *tanha* (craving; literally, hunger or thirst), namely, *bhava tanha* (wanting to get, be, and become what one likes), and *vibhava tanha* (wanting to get rid of what one dislikes). Today, a proper interpretation of this Middle Way implies avoiding greed-based consumerist tendencies on the one hand, and on the other hand it also implies avoiding world- and self-negative tendencies.

Additionally, in the second teaching, the *Anattalakkhana* [Characteristics of Non-self] *Sutta*, we find:

> The instructed noble disciple grows disenchanted with the body, disenchanted with feelings ... disenchanted he becomes

dispassionate. Through dispassion he is released. With release there is the knowledge of freedom and he discerns that [future re-]birth is exhausted, the Holy Life fulfilled, the task done. There is nothing further for this world.

It is important to note that disenchantment and dispassion here are rightly understood as an absence of enchantment, delusion, intoxication, and passion related to both greed/lust and hatred.

The position of the adult son of Buddhist parents expresses a superficial but all too common understanding of the Four Noble Truths and the teaching of non-self in Buddhism. It misses the key elements as well as the culminating effective discovery of the Buddha's enlightenment, *the Middle Way*—the Truth of the Path of Practice—the Noble Eightfold Path mentioned above. At the end of the aforementioned *Anattalakkhana Sutta*, we find that, upon hearing this teaching, the group of the first five *bhikkhus*—rather than becoming depressed—were delighted.

The Four Noble Truths contain the key functional elements of the paradigmatic shift that the Buddha experienced during his awakening and expressed in his first teaching. This new paradigm became the matrix for his entire teaching and path and may be rightly summarized as follows:

1. suffering is to be understood—thoroughly comprehended;
2. the causes of suffering are to be abandoned or discontinued;
3. the ending of suffering is to be realized and experienced;
4. there is a Path to do so.

When people do not sufficiently understand the Fourth Noble Truth, they can be utterly blindsided. Blindsiding the Path leads to neglecting the Third Noble Truth: the release from suffering. Then people begin to hope for the ending of suffering in some other imagined place and time, such as after death in another more wonderful dimension, rather than here and now. These ideas can make people feel disempowered or incapable of acting in the present world, rather than affirmed and empowered to cultivate, develop, and find fulfillment and happiness for themselves and for the world in which we now live.

According to classical Buddhist teaching, it is this world—our world—that is the ideal environment for enlightenment. This then is the right basis of Buddhist faith and optimism: human beings are able to realize and fulfill the Path and experience the fruits of this practice in this life for their benefit and for the benefit of all the world. This is what the Buddha compassionately taught. It is very important for a proper understanding of Right Effort. With proper Right Effort, our thoughts, words, and deeds are purified and elevated to forms of action that benefit all beings.

After enlightenment, the Blessed One himself walked for thirty-five years using his purified and liberated mental, verbal, and physical energies for the welfare of humanity. Not only did he do this himself, but, from the founding of his sangha to the day that he passed into ultimate Peace, he directed his disciples to do the same with the words:

> *Khaya vaya dhamma sankhara, apamadena sampadetha*
> Phenomenal things are subject to passing away.
> Become consummate through non-complacency.

His very last words are also often translated as "strive on with heedfulness." From the very first teaching to the last, the Buddha exhorted us in Right Effort, not with attachment and aversion, but by becoming consummate with the qualities of awareness, loving-kindness, compassion, appreciation, equanimity, and release. This is the very antithesis of the deadness, apathy, and complacency that may lead to nonaction and lack of interest in the state of the environment.

The majority of Western Buddhist monastics that I have met in the United States and elsewhere are making sincere efforts in their monastic lives to follow and live the Buddha's teaching as they understand it. We have good intentions, and we understand intention to be the fundamental or foundational karma since all words and actions arise from our mind informed by our intentions.

So in applying the Dharma today, the first work that we undertake is purifying our intentions. We purify greed by seeing its danger, by restraint, renunciation, and generosity. We purify ill-will by loving-kindness, compassion, and appreciation. We purify delusion through the ardent practice of mindfulness and full awareness as well as by looking into both the mind and mental and physical processes in a concentrated and illuminating way. But having good intentions is not the same as having knowledge of what is wholesome and unwholesome, as being wise and skillful. We must go deeper into the teaching of the Buddha to apply it properly.

In the mindfulness teaching so popular in Buddhist Insight Meditation, *sati* or mindfulness is taught hand in hand with *sampajanna* (clear comprehension or full awareness), within the timeframe of *atapi* (that is, dedicated and ardent consistency in applying oneself to the practice). It has been said that there is no real mindfulness or recollection without clear awareness or clear comprehension, and that there is no clear comprehension without recollection and mindfulness.

Looking into the definition of *sampajanna*, or clear comprehension, we come up with the question: clear comprehension of what? The nuts and bolts of the "what" is defined as a fourfold progression. This is clear comprehension and full awareness of:

1. What is intrinsically wholesome/skillful and unwholesome/ unskillful;
2. what is wholesome/skillful or not, according to time, place, and person;
3. what resources in our practical knowledge of the *Dhamma* are suitable/matching to resort to and to apply in the circumstance;

4. Through the nonconfusion/nondelusion that arises from the above three, becoming progressively and then fully and completely undeluded/unconfused.

This is the matrix for clear comprehension and full awareness in action. With these tools and resources, we are now able to consider how rightly to apply the Buddha's teachings to our particular modern contexts.

Here are some of the areas of concern in contemporary Buddhist monastic life that others have raised and that I have become aware of. I list them for the sake of recognition, acknowledgment, reflection, and consideration for wise response.

+ International and national jet travel and car travel by Buddhist monastics (carbon imprint)
+ The acceptance of nonvegetarian food as alms (carbon imprint, indirect harm toward other living beings, pollution, wasteful use of resources)
+ The use of existing waste management systems (pollution/ waste of energy and resources)
+ The use of existing electrical systems (pollution/waste)
+ The use of imported products offered as alms (pollution/ waste)
+ The use of chemical dyes for dying robes (pollution)
+ The acceptance of alms food and water in plastic and other environmentally harmful packaging (pollution, waste, and harmfulness to health)
+ The acceptance of more alms food than is needed for the monastic community (waste of resources)
+ The use of non–environmentally friendly requisite products offered as alms (pollution/waste)
+ The use of non–environmentally friendly cleaning products in monasteries (pollution and harmfulness to health)

- ✦ The construction or remodeling of monasteries using non–environmentally skillful technologies (pollution/waste), for example, not using solar, geothermal, wind, or water energy or water recycling systems, or making grandiose buildings with high roofs that waste energy to heat and cool
- ✦ The use of already existing unskillful/harmful technologies (pollution/waste)

From the list above, I will choose a few of the topics for specific and general introspection.

For Buddhist monastics in America, an issue related to environmental pollution (carbon) repeatedly raised is that of jet and car travel. This modern monastic practice is normally justified by appealing to the Buddha's injunctions to his monastic community to travel—even far and wide—in order to share and spread the *Dhamma* among those with eyes to see; to go to learn the *Dhamma*; and to exert oneself in finding suitable places to practice well and good companions in the Holy Life. Additionally there are teachings on the benefits to individual members of the monastic community and to the monastic community itself (as well as to other humans) of gathering often in harmony.

In the Buddhist monastic discipline of the *Vinaya*, monastics are enjoined to walk, rather than to ride in animal- or human-drawn vehicles, unless they happen to be ill. We understand this injunction to have been given so as not to burden or harm any other living beings, animal or human. Another reason for walking rather than riding is not to destroy the smaller forms of life that are so difficult for larger moving vehicles to avoid. Jain monastics in India still hold to this walking practice.

In earlier modern times we had imagined that coal- or gas-run vehicles did not burden or harm any living beings, and thus Buddhist monastics began to use such modes of transportation more and more widely. Now only a few maintain the old walking practice, and perhaps even then only for limited special periods of renunciate *dhutanga* (Thai: *tudong*) practice. However, the extensive harm done by such vehicular use is rapidly becoming more and more apparent.

Monastics who drive may feel that necessity or benefit outweighs the harm. I regard this weighing of harm and benefit as questionable. Those of us who accept cooked meat from an animal not killed for us as alms food sometimes use a similar argument for riding in a car: we are not the main cause of the harmful/painful action. "The plane will be flying anyway." But what of the monastery van? It is a carbon-emitting, polluting form of transportation, and it unavoidably harms smaller creatures.

We should not forget that monastics who have kept the walker's practice are powerful and inspiring examples of virtue to the world. The example of the *tudong* monks in Thailand has been a great inspiration for me. The opportunity to walk in this way in Thailand's northeast is one of the happiest and richest memories of my monastic life. In this walking practice, there was such a sense of release and freedom, of heightened awareness and flowing in the *Dhamma*, along with a sense of grace, of communion with the great monastic saints of old, and of closeness to the heart of the Buddha himself.

But walking in Asia, where the practice is known, supported, and revered, is not nearly as radical an act as walking in the United States. Walking for an extended period of time on the streets and highways of our country can help us see and know the actions of our society in a whole new way. It provides us with a sometimes harsh but very real awakening.

I have found this walking practice to be extremely efficacious for breaking through the veil of illusion produced by the myth of the car and the freedom (or is it slavery?) it gives us in this modern culture. Not using a car brings to the forefront the broiling issues that are just under the surface in our society. Not using money, and walking rather than driving—these small and simple things really do go radically and directly against the worldly stream. Actions like this call the entire

American way of life and system of values into question, and do so in a highly proactive but quiet, peaceful, and nonaggressive way.

In our women's monastic discipline, at least once a year barring illness we are required to relinquish our lodging and to make such a walk. Most modern *bhikkhunis* believe that going at least the minimum distance in a car or by bus or plane meets the requirement. However, I am again happy to call this interpretation into question. Although some may say that this is simply a point of mundane practicality, I would both agree and disagree. In its practicality and mundaneness, walking practice can cut to the chase—into what is deep, sublime, and profound—by showing us the world unveiled, without fabrication.

The majority of the concerns listed above relate to our livelihood as *bhikkhus* and *bhikkhunis*—alms mendicants—in Buddhist monastic life. With regard to our robes, our food and water, our lodging, and our medicines, we understand that the Buddha teaches monastics to practice equanimity and nonchoosing, nongrasping and nonstriving for personal worldly gain. For the wandering, walking, homeless alms mendicant, it is a fully appropriate and blessed practice to deepen one's renunciation through accepting whatever is offered or not offered with equanimity. Such a *samana's* steps are truly light for the world today.

In our modern Western society, however, the vast majority of Buddhist monastics live in more settled monasteries where wise choices may be made and where people may be taught, instructed, and guided in wise view, wise action, and wise livelihood. In this modern context too, our monastic discipline gives good examples, guidance, and precedents for not accepting too much and not accepting what is harmful to other human or nonhuman beings. In this regard, Buddhist monasteries such as Birkin Forest Monastery, Abhayagiri Monastery, Sravasti Abbey, and Shasta Abbey offer inspiring and uplifting examples.

However, one has to admit that the vast majority of our ethnic Asian Buddhist monasteries in North America often follow prevalent Western social norms. These behaviors are regularly reported to cause doubt, grief, and disappointment in the hearts of ecologically minded and newly converted Buddhists.

The precepts of our Buddhist monastic discipline in the *Vinaya* ask us to be conscientious about the waste put out from a Buddhist monastery. If we are to follow fully the monastic discipline, we are not to put out waste in such a way that we pollute the water, the earth, or "the green." Nor are we to use fire beyond what is medically necessary, especially if it means the harm and disturbance of other living beings.

One of my mentors in monastic life, the vice president of the Council of Thai Bhikkhus in the United States, the Venerable Ajahn Maha Prasert Kavissaro, recommended that I specifically mention the following point. In *Vinaya*, we are required to leave the toilet area as clean as or cleaner than when we entered. This precept is also extended to our use of monastic lodgings and furnishings, as well as to other public and private spaces in the monastery and to the places where we may camp in the wilderness while traveling or living as hermits. Additionally, unless invited by our hosts to do otherwise, this practice also extends to our behavior when visiting public places and lay homes outside the monastery. To do otherwise can do harm to the minds of others—to their faith in the Buddha, his teachings, and the sangha. It shows the offending monk's entrenchment in *samsara* and counters the teaching of gratitude and compassion. So, we must design our monasteries in a way that supports the *Vinaya* values concerning the cleanliness of our environment.

The Buddha's teaching may rightly be seen as very high, deep, and profound, tending to what is supermundane, peaceful, and beyond the world. We also find that the profound teaching of the Middle Way and the Buddhist Path of Practice relates directly to the practical issues of our worldly lives—to the mundane and to the material— even at the most elemental level. This holds true from the level of our views and intentions through to our livelihood and all of our efforts, and their wise application, both in lay and monastic life.

The moral and spiritual qualities commended by the Buddha: *samvega* (urgency), *hiri-ottapa* (a recognition of the harm that we have done and the wish to not further perpetuate it), and the Fourth Noble Truth of the Path of Practice (including Right View of cause and effect, Right Intention, Right Action, Right Effort, and Right Mindfulness in the teachings of *sati-sampajanna*—mindfulness and full awareness) all clearly stand out as highly relevant and appropriate teachings to be taught and practiced as we face our contemporary environmental crises.

Whatever our faults, we should bring the light of awareness to shine upon them, review them rightly according to the Buddhist teaching, and work proactively to reduce and eliminate them. Whatever our strengths and our wholesome, wise, and skillful resources, we should urgently and dedicatedly do everything in our power to develop and establish them. With joy and gladness for the goodness and effectiveness of this Path, with clarity and steady dedication, we must do this as if our very lives and livelihood depend on it, as this is the truth of the matter—not only for ourselves but for all living beings.

> *May we be well and happy, peaceful and at ease. May no harm come to us; may no danger come to us. May all beings be free from all suffering. May we not be parted from the good fortune we have attained. All beings are the owners of their actions, heirs to their actions, companions to their actions, dependent on their actions. Whatever we do, for good or for evil, to that will we fall heir.*

Complicity and Conversion

Fr. Hugh Feiss, OSB

As we undertake an exploration of the ecological shadow cast by our lives and the dark places of our hearts from which that shadow emerges, we can recall Indra's Net. If each of us is a crystal pearl that reflects all else, then we reflect the environmental blindness and harmful activities of all. We are, in fact, not just affected or stamped by their actions; in many, if not most instances, we are complicit in them. We might just think about the food we serve—the little packets of jam, the bananas transported from faraway lands, the plastic cups and plates. We might also think of our clothes that do not seem to be quite what Benedict had in mind when he spoke of locally available, inexpensive garments that could be handed on to the poor.

In what follows I will use "we" to refer to those of us who feel complicit in the environmental sins of our society. Perhaps you will not feel you are part of that "we," but if you do, I think "we" can come in the end to a confession or at least to a lament of how much we need to change if we are to be at home with all that is in God's beautiful world, and how much we probably cannot change and so how unfree and complicit we remain.

The topic is not a cheerful one, but we can start on a cheerful note. Monastics have many deep affinities with environmental stewardship. Our theory and practice commit us to dispossession and self-discipline—to asceticism. Our profession is designed to nurture virtue, reverence and care—ethics. Our way of life is ordered toward an abiding sense of the divine presence and at-one-ment with the divine—mysticism. And so the purposes and practices of our way of life provide a threefold impetus toward environmental living: ascetical, ethical, and mystical.[1] Or, better, our asceticism, ethics, and mystical awareness are three ways in which we become free in and for God, one another, and the world. Or again, they are three ways in which we are attuned to reality.

By this threefold practice we are formed to do a threefold service of sacramental worship, compassionate service, and witness. Our lifestyle (*conversatio*) should attune us to the sacramental depth of the physical world and so fit us for liturgy. The simplicity and disciplines of our life enable us to serve the needs of others. The presence of our communities can witness to the primacy of God, the mystery of every creature, "the dearest freshness deep down things," in the words of poet Gerard Manley Hopkins. So what keeps us from being more environmentally responsible, from being better witnesses?

It is possible to find peculiar theological justifications for not caring more wholeheartedly for the earth. None of them seems to be exclusively monastic, though I have known at least one monk who has voiced each of them. One is that the world is going to end anyway; in fact, we seem to be on the brink of destroying it. So why worry about the Lahontan trout, the level of mercury in the reservoir, or the trash in our dumpster? We are all going to die anyway, and the whole biosphere is going to die as well.

A second ideological trap is the domination model. There is a crass version: the world is ours to dominate, so we can do with it what we want. A more subtle form: we are the summit of creation and if it is a choice between "them" and us, "they" have to go. If cougars occasionally kill human beings, cougars must be exterminated. Both domination models assume that the world was made exclusively for humankind. But perhaps it has other purposes independent of our own.

A third ideological tool is moderation, the middle way. In her commentary on the Rule of Benedict, St. Hildegard emphasizes that Benedict set the bar neither too high nor too low. In English, my metaphor is ambiguous; it could be the bar on a high jump or the bar with stools in a tavern. Hildegard's illustration is equally ambiguous. She says that St. Benedict put the spigot in the barrel neither too high nor too low—which suggests moderate height, but would also make it easier to overindulge.

A fourth ideological illusion is the notion that because we are "contemplatives," we ought not to concern ourselves with the material world. This is closely connected with another bit of bad theology: contempt for the world (*contemptus mundi*), a phrase that occurs very frequently in medieval monastic authors. It is bad theology if it is interpreted to mean contempt for material things or shunning of created beauty and pleasure or even of creation as such. Or it could mean contempt for the greed that earthly things arouse in us.

So much for the theological justifications for our environmental irresponsibility. There are some other ideological traps into which we fall, not through skewed theology, but through the impact of our culture. These are subtle and pervasive. If one takes *contemptus mundi* to mean disdain for the seductions of desire occasioned by the culture around us, perhaps we could use a bit more of it. Ours is a culture based on the seduction of marketing and advertising. If, as studies have shown, the average American boy spends only minutes (at best) of "quality time" with his father each day, that same boy spends four or five hours plugged into electronic media, and many other hours in the company of peers who are saturated with the "affluenza" virus. If his family are practicing Catholics he spends one hour a week in church and maybe another in religious education class. Christian monasteries exist for those who want to spend hours a day with their heavenly Father and their lives with others who share Christ's teaching. The consumerist bacillus reaches us nonetheless. We cannot avoid exposure, but we can inoculate ourselves by immersing ourselves in the worldview held by our cognitive minority and recognizing the difference between our worldview and the worldview of the consumer culture.

A second cultural trap is mistaking good intentions for actual internal and external change. Many denizens of Western places like Sun Valley and Aspen are green: they go to environmental lectures, contribute to the Nature Conservancy, buy organic eggs and milk, and drive a Prius. They oppose light and noise pollution in their communities—and go to sleep with a sense of environmental righteousness in their McMansions that leave an environmental footprint the size of an aircraft carrier. We monks need to do what we say.

A third cultural trap is pragmatism. Male monastics are sometimes a bit defensive about being practical. Often their experience of the world is somewhat limited, or if they entered the monastery later in life, they regard their fellow monks who entered the community at an early age as impractical. In either case, they are liable to reject proposals to adopt more environmentally friendly practices as impractical, chimeras dreamt up by people who are out of touch with the real world or—in Idaho parlance—seduced by New England liberals. One form of this pragmatism is the sort of stewardship that argues that people have given us money or we have earned it, and we need to be good stewards of that money, which means we invest or spend it most economically—without reference to externalities. Then we cannot afford to put in solar heating, because it will not pay for itself in fewer than nineteen years.

Thus far we have spoken of theological and cultural illusions that can justify bad practices. I think that to these we might—with apologies to Anna Freud—add a third category of psychological ploys. These are ways we cope with horrific or inconvenient truths. They help us live the contradictions between our convictions and claims and the compromises and complicities to which we are party. Denial is one. A woman, whose husband works for the dairy industry, told me that science is inconclusive about the effects of bovine growth hormones and the regular use of low-level doses of antibiotics in industrial dairies. We can say to ourselves: anthropogenic global warming has not been proven. Or we can fail to face the fact that we are not doing more in defense of the environment because we are afraid to alienate our supporters and constituents.

A second defense mechanism is repression, by which we bury our awareness of our responsibilities for the impacts of our actions and lifestyle.

A third mechanism is projection: China is producing x-million tons of greenhouse gasses per year, so what difference does it make if we run our two-stroke lawnmowers or drive to the post office instead of riding a bike there?

During this encounter, we have discussed how theology and monastic tradition and experience can alleviate the ecological crisis in which we find ourselves. It has been my sad task to ponder ways in which we monks can avoid letting the ecological crisis cast light on our monastic lifestyles and call us to a deeper embrace of the ethical, ascetical, and mystical fabric of our lives in which we seek at-one-ment and attunement with God, one another, and God's world, which we share.

Let me end by pushing back beyond false ideologies and doctrines to two primordial ways of being in the world, which illustrate the stark options that face humanity and highlight the contribution we can make to meeting the environmental challenge.

> The world is will. But not divine or human will; it is not something with an intention, a direction, an aim, or a plan. It is just a blind, aimless, purposeless, all-powerful force on which everything depends but which itself depends on nothing or no one. . . . Thus the whole world of phenomena is a constant, endless struggle of all against all, as each battles to survive at the cost of the rest of the world. . . .[2]

That is the way a contemporary philosopher sums up the thought of Schopenhauer. If one splices in a "selfish gene" it seems to be the way many evolutionary biologists (not to mention MBAs) think the world works. Such a picture offers no reason except self-interest to care about the effects of our actions on the world or much hope that we can make a difference. And self-interest is what precipitated us into our current situation; it is unlikely to save us.

By contrast, here is an excerpt from a poem by Margaret Avison:

> Every living thing
> as a mass or a
> morsel or one who moves with
> the speed of light—
> each in His miracle of particularity
> the Lord knows.[3]

What science and our religious traditions tell us is that everything in its God-given particularity is interconnected with everything else. We seek at-one-ment or enlightenment as part of a whole to which and for which we are responsible. For the health and protection of that whole and each thing within it, we monks can contribute vision, motivation, and practices that are at once ethical, ascetical, and mystical. If we turn toward the earth with reverence and care, we can be confident that we will find its Ground and Goal. I am not sure we can do that if we do not confess and lament our complicity in the illusions that have brought us to the current crisis.

Good Practices, Ancient and Emerging

Good Practices of Buddhist Monastic Communities in North America

Ven. Thubten Semkye

The Buddha did not give teachings on world environmental issues. Twenty-six hundred years ago, there were seas of jungle with wild animals and only small islands of civilization. The earth was not encumbered by humanity; she held all beings quite easily.

Nonetheless, I think one can safely say that the Buddha was the most brilliant, astute environmentalist in the history of our world. He focused not on the outer environment but on the ecology of the inner life. After seeing old, ill, and dead people—as well as a wandering ascetic—for the first time, he began to explore the origin of suffering as well as the path that freed one from suffering. The Buddha identified and eliminated the poisons (attachment, anger, and delusion) within his own mind that caused his suffering. With the pollution removed, the vast, clear, and knowing nature of his mind was revealed. This restoration of his inner ecosystem illuminated the virtuous qualities within his mind to a radiant perfected state.

With this restored vast and open mind, imbued with all the virtuous qualities we can only imagine, he walked the world. Those who were inspired and compelled to emulate him became the first monastics. He taught them with this inner ecology field guide (the Four Noble Truths, the Eightfold Path or the Three Higher Trainings) in order to help them nourish and sustain their inner lives so they could live harmoniously with one another and with the world. The commitment of the sangha from then until now, twenty-six hundred years later, has kept the Buddha's inner habitat restoration field guide alive and well and in its pure form.

The beauty of this practice of inner ecology is that it is shared by other spiritual traditions, especially with regard to the practices of compassion, interdependence, and simplicity, which are not exclusive to any one religion, or, in fact, to religion as such. His Holiness the Dalai Lama includes them in all his talks on secular ethics.

Now that Buddhism has come to the West, Buddhist monastics in the United States and Canada are continuing this beautiful lineage of inner sustainability in their communities. Our commitment to practice ethical discipline, to live simply, to experience the interdependence of all things, to be mindful and content—and at the same time to be innovative and extremely creative thinkers who look outside the box of what the world believes is possible in regard to the planet—is already happening. It is simple yet profound.

We monastics have the most conducive circumstances to bring about this kind of life, and we can then share what we are doing with those who meet us, learn about us, and are inspired by us. They can then look toward their own innate good hearts and find the deep wisdom to restore their own inner environments to that pure state. We want to model for them a happy life without an excessive lifestyle.

But the world today, as we well know from our own experience of working on our minds, is more complicated than in the Buddha's time. The distractions and cravings are more numerous, the fear and anxiety more prevalent.

Michael Pollan, writing for the *New York Times Magazine*, published an article called "Why Bother?" in which he states that our culture is going through not only a crisis of lifestyle but also a crisis of character.[1] The inner environment of many Westerners (and, in my view, of Americans in particular) is stressed from the poison of intense dissatisfaction and craving. Pollan states, "Virtue these days is a term of derision, or liberal soft headedness. For a culture that prides itself on individualism, we are conformists continually trying to fit into our culture's view of success or fame. The sum total of everyday choices made mostly by us (the consumer who contributes seventy percent to the economy) is mostly made in the name of our needs, desires and preferences."

I believe the outer environmental crisis has come to this critical point because our inner environment is so disturbed, agitated, and smoldering. Reining in our desires is seen as unpatriotic and oppressive. "I want what I want when I want it" has become the mantra of our culture. Virtuous lifestyles that reflect contentment, simplicity, and ethical discipline seem out of date in the face of our culture's high-speed greed and its addiction to success, sense pleasures, and reputation.

There is hope, however; models for a new paradigm are emerging. I have gathered some wonderful examples of Buddhist monastic communities in the United States and Canada that live within a spiritual ecosystem and support, by their example, the well-being of others outside that system. They live simply, yet are unafraid to try what many naysayers say is too difficult, too restrictive, or too late. What follows here is based on responses to a questionnaire I sent to Buddhist monasteries asking what their communities are doing in terms of good inner and outer environmental practices.

1. What Buddhist principles or teachings has your monastery translated into environmental practices for ways of doing things within daily community life, and in terms of your building structures, use of resources, care of the land?

All the monasteries I contacted practice simplicity of lifestyle or the ethics of frugality. Carpooling by community members as well as lay supporters is highly encouraged. Each of the communities recycles stringently, and repairs and reuses wood, metal, appliances, and furniture. Sravasti Abbey guides its supporters when they donate food, encouraging them out of respect for the environment to purchase minimally packaged items. The food offerings are brought in cloth grocery bags rather than in plastic or paper bags.

Abhayagiri Forest Monastery encourages its supporters not to buy bottled water since their well water at the abbey is quite good. The manufacturing of plastics is environmentally unhealthy and when liquid is heated or frozen in the bottles, poisons are released.

All the monasteries depend on the kindness of others and eat only what is offered. They are also prudent with the monetary offerings given to them, and the monastics have few personal possessions.

All the communities practice harmlessness and protecting life, seeing all living things as worthy of care and respect. Bhavana Forest Monastery uses Have-a-Heart traps and other creative nonviolent techniques that minimize harm to living things such as snakes, yet keep the residents safe.

All the monasteries eat a vegetarian diet. Sravasti Abbey purchased a ewe and her two lambs when it was discovered that a neighbor would be butchering them. They found them a home with a vegetarian shepherdess who was looking to add to her flock for wool spinning.

Each of the monasteries has unique forest stewardships for their lands. Bhavana sees their monastery as a "precious jewel in the green forest." They are currently trying to prevent the Allegheny Power Company from building a new two-hundred-foot-wide right-of-way through the forest adjacent to their property to install a new 500 kV transmission line. They are encouraging the company to use instead an already existing right-of-way further down the road and double stack the wires on taller towers to preserve acres of undisturbed forest.

Birken Forest Monastery in Canada has an eighty-acre bird sanctuary that is left undisturbed without structures on it. They also leave the fallen wood to decompose and for habitat. Sravasti Abbey uses the dead standing wood in their forest for firewood and has begun an ambitious project of thinning areas of their 240-acre property for fire safety.

Both Birken and Abhayagiri use solar power for their electricity needs and Abhayagiri is hoping to decrease its use of propane for heat in the near future. Sravasti Abbey will be using a geothermal system to heat the new monastic residence that is being built this year.

Finally all feel that silent or solitary retreats for their community members are crucial for the individual's inner ecology.

2. What individual or group patterns or ways of thinking have been the most challenging for the community to change in its efforts to live what the Buddha taught?

All the communities responded that members find it hard to break conditioned consumer habits, and that restraint, although not easy, does help conserve resources. Novices are older now and have built up life patterns that can be challenging to change. Younger community members, who have been raised in a disposable culture, do not think of repairing appliances, computers, or printers. Rather, they put them in a closet and suggest that new ones be bought. Another challenge is for community members to look on the tools and supplies at the monastery as if they were their own and to treat them with care.

Shasta Abbey feels that green office and cleaning supplies help take care of the planet, but they warn of a kind of green snobbery that may arise if communities are not careful. Supplies offered with a pure heart should be used. The residents at Sravasti Abbey educate their lay supporters in the use of green cleaning supplies, thereby helping everyone transition away from environmentally harsh products.

3. What role in the environmental movement do you see the Buddhist monastic community playing in inspiring and influencing the lay public at the grassroots level as well as the larger connection through writings, internet, and teachings?

Abhayagiri believes that many monastics are well educated about global warming, although not outspoken. Birken Forest Monastery holds a Green Monday where lay supporters and the monastics have group discussions about ecology and care for the planet. The teaching on dependent origination, says Bhavana, can help people see how everything arises due to causes and conditions and that there is a rippling effect in all that we do. The forest monasteries also see themselves as "refuges of green." It was not for lack of buildings that the Buddha himself was born, attained enlightenment, and passed away in *parinirvana*, all out in nature and underneath a tree. There is a hidden message here: that the vibrations of nature have a subtle, healing effect on our minds. The forests can teach us so much about life. The Buddha's example should encourage us to try to preserve as much of the rapidly depleting natural environment as we can. That should be the message and mission of the forest monasteries—to serve as refuges and to be the last bastions against the onslaught of rampant materialism threatening to swallow up the islands of green.

Shasta Abbey and Sravasti Abbey both feel that lay practitioners look to the monastics for help in coping with our fast-spinning modern world. They watch us to see how we do things and how we deal with the world.

Sravasti Abbey has held a retreat on environmentalism. Ven. Thubten Chödrön, the abbess of Sravasti Abbey, incorporates environmental issues in many of her teachings and has written about it in her book *Path to Happiness*.[2] One of the main points she makes is that "us versus them, friend versus enemy" polarizations can be huge obstacles to positive change.

The responses to my questionnaire show that Buddhist monastic communities in the United States and Canada are not only integrating the Buddha's field guide of good environmental practices on the inside; they are also translating them to the outside. This is not to say that we do not have a lot of work to do. There are still many issues that we have to work through. How do we feed large groups of people without filling bags with Styrofoam and nonreusable plastics? How much driving do our kind lay supporters do to make up for the driving we do not do? What forums are appropriate for monastics as far as sharing and networking with the public around the environment? What can we learn from others? How do we connect with the world where our practice and lifestyles could be used as role models for others?

These questions will be answered as time goes on, and the Buddhist monastic communities will confront these issues as they arise. May we all benefit from their efforts and example.

Good Practices of Catholic Monastic Communities in North America

Sr. Renée Branigan, OSB

Anyone familiar in the least with the Rule of Benedict will know that good stewardship is endemic to its spirit. However, not everyone who meets a follower of the Rule or appears on the monastery doorstep has actually read the text of the Rule. Instead they read the environment and practices; they listen to our vocabulary and tone; they observe how and what we acquire, use, and dispose. Those of us who profess to follow Benedict tremble occasionally when we recognize that we are such public, even if sometimes unintentional, preachers. This is perhaps especially true when we are in buildings too big, too old, too inefficient that we cannot simply disencumber by good intentions. We have personal habits that we do not remember acquiring but that we now seriously want to unlearn. We reach for our Rule of Benedict for comfort; it is a "little rule for beginners" (chapter 73), and that is what we are.

Every Catholic monastic community that started out in America had the same initial plan: make do. Most communities had early days of poverty ranging from dire to not so bad, and those were the days that were probably the most environmentally friendly in our history. Poverty makes it pretty easy to keep your ear to the ground and your face to the wind. In times when you have little, stewardship and stewardship of nature are somewhat synonymous. But as our communities built and accumulated, perhaps we became a bit careless and insulated with comfort and convenience. The terms diverged a bit, so when we spoke of stewardship we were most likely speaking of "our" resources, those we had accumulated for our use and dispensation rather than those of our planet, present for sharing with all.

This divergence has proven costly both to our spirits and to our purses. Now the pinch to our purses is offering a gift to our spirits. Many of us who find ourselves going green now are doing so because we cannot afford to do otherwise, but once we are on that course we are spiritually restored by its wisdom and "run with hearts expanded" (Rule of Benedict, prologue). As Bertolt Brecht observes, "Terrible is the seductive power of goodness." The point I am making is that most of us started out environmentally friendly by necessity, strayed as we became more established and comfortable, and now, I propose, are looking again to renewed friendliness out of a tight blend of fiscal necessity and good ecological intentions, but we find it more costly and complicated.

Last October, when I sent out a call in the *American Monastic Newsletter* for those who had made ecologically driven decisions, I was not overwhelmed with responses, but I did get some good ones. I would like to preface this section with three observations: first, we can assume, I am absolutely sure, that all communities embrace environmental stewardship as a core value, but the degree to which they live that value varies; second, I am equally sure that communities want and strive to do more; and a minor third, it is just as well I did not hear from more communities than I did because I want to acknowledge the distinct contributions of each of those who did respond. Here are some highlights from those who opened their doors to us.

The first community I heard from was the Benedictine Sisters of Perpetual Adoration in Clyde, Missouri. Even with the encumbrances of aging buildings, their commitment to preserving the planet has found expression in creative and substantial ways. Whether deconstructing buildings or small fans, the dismantling for other use is pretty total. As with the Amish, what was old and useless in its former life becomes useful, fashioned into art or awning, recycled as scrap metal, and so forth. Here, "nothing is wasted" is truer than in most places.

In addition they have shifted priorities in the use of their land. The two-hundred-plus acreage they had leased for income from crops is now home to native grasses and wildflowers as part of the U.S. Department of Agriculture's Conservation Reserve Program designed to reduce soil erosion and enhance the environment. Wildlife abounds here too. The sisters (maybe not all of them) extend the Benedictine rule of hospitality, "Greet all as Christ," even to the mice and bats they catch and relocate. Bats are entitled to their own lodgings because they earn their keep by devouring insects in the humid Missouri summers.

And finally, a 289-foot wind turbine on their property benefits the local energy cooperative but not the sisters directly because of a federal law that does not permit switching utilities. It does meet their goals, however, of contributing to the local community and promoting wind energy.

The second community is that of the Sisters of Immaculata Monastery in Norfolk, Nebraska. After two years of considering their gifts and energies for ministry, they divested themselves of their hospitals and focused more on the spiritual offerings at their home monastery. They are in the process of renovating their monastery built in 1964, and one of their primary values was recycling. Of the one hundred loads of debris, more than ninety were completely recycled and the rest were partially so. The walls and concrete products are taken for use as filler for building and reinforcing roads. All metals that can be recycled are taken for new construction. They have asked that in their new construction as much recycled material be used as possible, thus closing the circle. The floors in the dining room and library will be made of cork, a natural product that does not require the destruction of the tree but merely the harvesting of the bark, which regenerates.

In addition to higher efficiency utilities, they are investigating ways to reclaim the condensation from the air-conditioning units to flow into a reservoir for their landscaping.

Their goal is not only to do as little damage to the planet as possible but also to educate and share their values with all who use their facility. Obviously their renovation continues to be as internal as it has been external, as their community involvement has been high. And as a P.S., because beauty is definitely environmentally friendly, they added a labyrinth!

We go to the East Coast for our third community: Portsmouth Abbey in Portsmouth, Rhode Island. This community of fifteen monks has a boarding school, and they too live and teach a strong message about the environment. After doing all the usual stuff, they installed the first utility-scale 660 kW wind turbine in the state of Rhode Island. Though paid for by the abbey with a partial grant from the state, it was a gift to their school, a gift that keeps on giving. It will pay for itself in four years, even as it generates small revenue in the kilowatt buyback from the utility company when more is generated than is used. That revenue is put into a fund to promote environmentally friendly projects in the school. Last fall they completed a green dormitory with solar hot water and heat assist, heat-recovery ventilation, spray foam insulation, and other green features.

They are in the process of erecting a solar house designed by a local university for the 2005 Solar Decathlon, a house that is entirely energy self-sufficient.

We come back to the Midwest for our fourth community, St. Mary Monastery in Rock Island, Illinois. When I saw all that Sister Phyllis, the prioress, sent me, I asked if we could have their house! She said no, but they would share it if I—or you—came to visit. This community had the "advantage" (I put quotes around that because home space is home space) of selecting a new location and new construction with at least some funds from the sale of their former monastery in

Nauvoo, Illinois. That would not be impressive if they did not make good environmental choices, but they did.

First, they built a right-sized place when they built in 1997. They had more numbers then, but they bought houses nearby for their larger numbers, and sold them as their numbers decreased. They even have a gradual exit strategy for their new monastery building, because it can be converted into a nursing home if necessary.

Second, they invested in geothermal heating and cooling, using pond loops in a five-acre pond that also serves as an environmentally friendly place for water run-off, drainage, and a natural habitat for fish and fowl. They have put fourteen acres into Illinois prairie grasses and wildflowers, and they preserve another eleven acres of fallow land and fifty acres of woodlands. Within the building they are going to install a green EcoSpace elevator, which uses traction rather than hydraulic fluid. Other than using a smaller motor and thus less electricity, it has no payback other than earth preservation, but the community deemed that it was worth the expense.

We are on the home stretch now, heading to the fifth (and my favorite) community, Sacred Heart Monastery on the plains in western North Dakota. We are presently in our second year of "right-sizing" a monastery building that is too large for us at present and most likely in the future. As we do everything by consensus, we move at a pace that makes it possible for all of us to move lovingly and wisely. We have to face some practicalities; despite our best intentions we are going to have to let go of some things that are still useful but that are not useful enough in their present state for us to maintain. We have crafted our vocabulary to articulate our actions rather than hide them: we are deconstructing for harvesting rather than demolishing. This is a hard sell, for we are a community that has known genuine poverty through the first half of our existence. We do not waste. Part of our dance through reality has been that, yes, we have this space and others do not, but while others could use it, there really is not a way to pick up a section of a well-built brick building and move it someplace else.

One of our key insights about our stand on the environment came in 1997 when Bishop Paul Zipfel of the diocese of Bismarck made his first visit to our monastery. As we were going around the dining room introducing ourselves and saying what we did, one of our older sisters said simply, "I'm Sister Jeanette Werner, and I save the world." She had taken over the responsibility of our recycling, and she took the job very seriously and reveled in it. What was stunning about her statement was that she got it; she had her eyes on the goal. She also clarified for us our focus and our aim.

Since the mid-1990s we have been involved with wind energy and erected the first commercial turbine in North Dakota. The story of how this project evolved over a five-year period would make for a good book or a movie, complete with a cast of unsavory characters and plot twists. But we had done our homework, and we knew someone had to take the risk for all of us in our area. We also knew that we had to do something about our rising electrical bills. So we plunged. We began producing electricity on June 16, 1997. We have saved money, of course, but there are greater benefits. We got a glowing report from the University of North Dakota because of the 1841 tons of CO_2 that we have offset in our first ten years. Better still, wind farms in our state are growing, and North Dakota, a state so rich in coal and oil (and so in the grip of those industries), is finally seriously thinking about other energy sources. We have allied ourselves more strongly and publicly with the Dakota Resource Council and have been identified as pro-environment because of our turbines. They serve as public testimony of our commitment and are the focal point of countless tours and talks.

Another smaller environmental statement we make is through our herd of llamas. God rather tricked us into this commitment, but it has paid us dividends we never anticipated. When we were first offered a couple of llamas, they were at their peak of their potential to make a good return on the dollar. We had the space and the climate; they are low-maintenance animals, so it was a no-brainer for us. Of course, right after we got into the business, the bottom dropped out of the market, but by then we were attached. Those llamas helped us back our way into organic farming—we use llama "soil enhancers" rather than chemicals in our garden. We also spin and dye their wool, and this has become quite a cottage industry for us. Several of our sisters knit, crochet, or felt items for sale. Llamas are real return-to-the-earth, peaceful animals and have done wonders for our spirits. They, too, are a great public attraction and offer an occasion for teaching.

I will close with five insights on positive American monastic environmental practices, listed randomly and based not only on the responses I received from the five communities who returned my questionnaire, but also on my reading, observing, and thinking over these last thirty years. These are obviously open for discussion or even refutation.

First, our hearts are good, but we are not nearly mindful enough in our behavior. It is not so much lack of education as lack of disciplined commitment—speed, convenience, busyness, and so on are seductive and too easily excusable.

Second, necessity is an actual grace and God is generous with it. Necessity will prompt us to be better stewards and perhaps to take bolder risks, but the action will still have to be ours. Economics may force the decision, but the good of the environment will definitely shape it.

Third, we are all doing something, and we can all do more, but as we do more, we cannot allow ourselves to be overwhelmed by all we are not yet doing. In an age and culture marked by speed and instant gratification, it isn't easy to see the value in bit-by-bit, steady progress, in doing what we can.

Fourth, good stewardship of the earth is inseparable from our promise of stability. While our community is our home, our home lives in a place, and we become especially responsible for that environment and how it ripples out. We cannot excuse ourselves from knowing our land and the politics that govern its future.

And fifth, because good ecology has become such an expensive venture in some of the larger, more long-term areas, it appears to create the false dilemma of conflicting with another promise we make: poverty. It's not right to say, "We cannot go fully green because we haven't enough gold." We need to shift the focus from economics to the deeper values of the environment and start there. We must be innovative, creative—and sacrificial.

I would like to leave you with an image. Think of a clothesline continuum of care and concern for the earth. The left end of the continuum represents less care and concern; the right, more. If we place American monastic communities on this continuum according to what they may think and feel, they will probably be clustered toward the right. When we ask the question about the long-term decisions our communities make that either affirm or renege on our care and concern for the earth, the distribution may be stretched even further along the continuum toward the left. And third, when we ask the question about daily behaviors of our communities and what it says about our care and concern, I dare say we would see the broadest distribution. This would be true, I think, if you did this same exercise within each individual community, and with each individual in community. This is not surprising; we will always have a gap between the desired and the real.

What has not seemed to happen on a larger scale, I think, has been an ignited desire to radically change the real. We are still beginners and our dreams seem sadly small. And yet, from these five communities (and there are many more who did not respond but who are doing remarkable things) I draw hope and inspiration from their commitment, action, teaching, and fire. These examples are graced accelerants. May they fan the flames of our desire to tend this gracious earth more lovingly.

VI

Epilogue: Insights from Dialogue

Challenges to Living a Green Spirituality

Birken

The Tradition of the Green Forest Monastery

Ajahn Sona

My early interest in Buddhism arose from a perception that a great deal of the ethic of Buddhism concerned the environment. I was impressed with the preservation of nature around the ancient Chinese and Japanese monasteries. Not only did I appreciate their precept not to kill human beings but also their astonishing commitment to the nonkilling, indeed nonharming, of animals. I had not come across it in any other society, contemporary or past. They had realized an ideal: they did not merely philosophize, nor was this limited to the occasional, eccentric hermit taking up a radical lifestyle of harmlessness. Rather, these were large, well-organized communities in which people lived their lives conscientiously adhering to this lofty aspiration. At the time, I must admit, I did not have much of a grasp of the higher spiritual motivation behind this behavioral ethic, but it was a fine gateway into understanding Buddhism. I think many of my generation—the boomers—may also have come to an interest in Buddhism through pacifism and environmentalism.

I want to stay on the topic of applied environmentalism in our Buddhist communities in this chapter, but I think it is important to realize that Buddhism creates a context around environmentalism—an attitude that lightens the self-polluting emotions of frustration, anger, and despair, which often fuel well-meaning environmentalists in the

West. Many of the best political and social organizations for the protection of the environment have arisen in the West, such as the Sierra
Club, World Wildlife Federation, and Greenpeace. Equivalent organizations are difficult to find in Asia. These necessary reactions to the
havoc wreaked by technology gone mad in the nineteenth and twen-
tieth centuries have arisen, perhaps unsurprisingly, in the very culture
that created the problem in the first place. People who are thoroughly
versed in science and technology, yet able to recognize how the inven-
tions of these enterprises can be perverted, have been the movers and
shakers behind the environmental movement. The critical leadership
that these people offer, though, needs to be supplemented by a healthier, non-self-destructive attitude that Buddhist meditative techniques
and philosophical attitudes can provide.

We are at a crossroads with such problems as global warming,
increasing cancer rates due to chemical saturation, psychological problems from urban overcrowding, and on, and on. All these signs point
to a right-angle turn on the road of the rapidly accelerating population
and related social revolutions of the last four hundred years. There is
a radical alternative that we are actually being forced to undertake,
and that, if ignored, threatens collapse and disaster on a scale without parallel in history. Therefore we need concrete, practical, idealistic communities in which it is proven that human nature can not
only function but thrive. I do not expect the entire world population
to suddenly become monks and nuns (!), but in the same way that
Olympic athletes motivate kids from the back of cereal boxes, humans
in general need idealists to motivate them. Humans need not only
threats and depressing news reports about environmental degradation but also inspiring, positive alternatives: the possibility of finding
(to borrow a Judeo-Christian image) a land of milk and honey.

Buddhist monastic communities can provide an example of a
twenty-five-hundred-year experiment in alternative communal living
that has actually worked. I have lived in a number of Buddhist communities over the last thirty years in the West and the East, both as a

lay participant and as a fully immersed monastic. This experience has taught me much about finding our way to simplicity and sufficiency, both in view of a community's practical organization as well as teaching and transmitting useful attitudes for it to be psychologically in harmony with these lifestyle choices. In order for monks and nuns to present a relevant message to the ordinary, idealistic, nonascetic layperson, our communities need to show viable ways for people to change their modes of living so as to be less damaging and more positive to the environment.

Our present community is set in the forest about an hour from the nearest significant town, close enough to be available to people who cannot dwell in the forest all the time. It is a place where many come for restoration and where they can learn to make changes in their own urban and suburban environments. At times I have lived in extremely primitive monasteries, without electricity, without running water, with outhouses, and using wood gathered by hand. Such a life is entirely feasible for seasoned monastics, but people who are raised with electric lights, flush toilets, and faucets that produce warm water are unlikely to find that lifestyle applicable in their own. So our community at Birken has many of the modern conveniences but few of the modern inconveniences. We have demonstrated that this can be done, and done relatively easily. Doing so can create a sanctuary for the diverse flora and fauna around us, and an emotional sanctuary for humans that does not require an excessive, frivolous use of resources to accomplish.

Although it would require a small book to do it justice, I shall now describe the specific technologies and practices of our monastery. We are "off-grid," that is, we are not connected to the state electricity grid. The nearest grid connection is four miles away. The cost of connecting to it would have been $175,000—economically out of the question for us. Thus, our involuntary journey into off-grid modernity. We have evolved quickly from the raw use of an overpowered and desperately inefficient diesel generator to producing electricity through a hybrid diesel generator-battery bank. This hybrid model is what makes the Prius such a fuel efficient car; it is also what makes diesel locomotives efficient. There have been diesel-electrics for sixty years. This was news to us, so part of our journey has been to rediscover the ingenuity of previous generations.

Moving off-grid stimulated a steep learning curve. We began examining each of the electrical appliances—lights, pumps, and so forth—in the monastery for their power consumption. By systematically reducing our consumption, we achieved an electrical usage per resident of the monastery that amounted to 10 percent of the average American! This astonished us because the sacrifices were virtually unnoticeable. As our efficiencies went up on a grand scale our appetite for further efficiency was only further whetted. The psychology of this experience, I think, is going to be part of a general tendency in society: once you venture in the direction of simplicity and sufficiency, the game becomes enjoyable and even addictive! We have computers (five!), plentiful electric light, toasters, coffee makers, a washing machine and dryer (though we now seldom use the dryer, preferring "air dryers" of the indoor and outdoor type). The monastery has excellent well water, which we pump ourselves. To save water we switched to dual-flush toilets. A urine flush requires only three quarts, and a major flush, about a gallon and a half. This is a drastic reduction without any hardship over conventional five-gallon toilets. Remember, this also reduces the electrical demand needed to pump the water from three hundred feet down. *Everything is connected.*

Our research has shown both that thoughtlessly purchased appliances are grossly inefficient and that this is neither accidental nor inevitable. To our initial surprise we realized that the same folks who make and sell electricity also make and sell the appliances. (They also give donations to political candidates.) This struck us as suspicious! With some in-depth reading we discovered an easily penetrated secret. After noticing that Europeans make far more efficient appliances we discovered that inefficiency in North America has been a deliberate policy. With such outfits as General Electric woven into the fabric of modern-day America, "planned obsolescence"—a government-instituted policy after the Second World War to increase sales—is not so noticeable when you are on the grid. That is why off-grid living is as much an economic and political revelation as it is an environmental adventure.

After reducing our electrical demands significantly, we began to concentrate on refining our electrical production. The scant wind resources and lack of significant falling water in our area mean that the only viable alternative to our diesel generator is the sun. Solar photovoltaic panels are a considerable investment. Although this fact initially sent us scurrying to our calculators, we have found that they are justified in the end, as the monastery quickly reduced its carbon footprint by fully 30 percent. This is the most expensive alternative energy at present, yet our tiny demand makes these electric costs quite reasonable.

We are now in our final phase of refinement. The involvement of our resident community and supporters makes this a concrete learning experience for everyone connected to the monastery. In addition, we publish these initiatives on the Web, so those who simply peruse our Web site for interest's sake can gain from our experience (this is why we have the computers). Phase 2 will consist of doubling our solar panels, using highly efficient water circulation pumps for heat, motion-sensor LED lights, and a highly efficient wood-fired water heater. We expect this to bring us close to our ultimate goal of 100 percent solar-generated electricity and 100 percent biofuel-generated heat. In our case, "biofuel" is a fancy word for *wood*, which we collect in the surrounding forests. As a pertinent aside, we live in British Columbia, which is larger than California, Oregon, and Washington combined. The BC forest is perhaps the largest pine forest in the world. It contains about 80 percent pine trees and, shockingly, most of them are dead. They have been killed in the last five years by an extraordinary infestation of pine beetles. The reason: global warming.

Until recently severe winters kept pine beetle populations at moderate levels. This stopped occurring ten years ago and has created an ecological disaster of world-class proportions. The small consolation we have is unlimited firewood, which if left unburned will return to atmospheric carbon in twenty years anyway. We are still pondering all the implications of this unprecedented disaster.

We still have not discussed transportation. It is perhaps strange to think of a Buddhist monk being fascinated with modern transportation. Not in the sense of enjoying cars or the "glamour" of air travel, but simply trying to apply the "simplicity and sufficiency" philosophy to the snarled and profoundly inefficient movement of humans and goods around the earth. We ourselves are condemned to transporting goods from the city to the country in a seven-passenger Toyota van. The monastery makes the best of the internal combustion engine, because at present there is no choice. We go to town as rarely as possible, as little as once a week; we pack the vehicle with people, groceries, and building supplies. And so we try to squeeze down our footprint. Ultimately, however, this will not do: the internal combustion engine must go. We eagerly follow the rapidly developing news of electric vehicles, which we will harness to our solar panels. We expect this to be the next significant step in our own low-impact journey. I often give talks about urban living, in which I advocate public transport, streetcars, electric trains, electric buses, good old bicycling—and, of course, walking. The more I discover about the chaotic and inefficient infrastructures of city transportation, the more I realize that the solutions are fairly simple but have been complicated by outright manipulation, greed, and corrupt politics.

In summary, our community puts a great deal of thought and effort into efficient, adequate housing, food, and transportation. Most of all, though, the monastery is devoted to an ongoing spiritual education in inward simplicity and sufficiency, in order to supply this great paradigm shift with the necessary, nontoxic, inner fuel.

The Monastic Challenge to Respond in Love

Sr. Anne McCarthy, OSB

There we were, the participants of the Gethsemane III Encounter on the Environment, having walked to a place honored by all of us: the hermitage of the monk Thomas Merton, early pioneer of Monastic Interreligious Dialogue, poet, mystic, spiritual teacher, and prophet. It was the right place for the ceremony, blessing, commitment, and dedication that closed our gathering. We had crafted and come to consensus on a statement to be offered to our communities and to the public. Looking out over quiet, lush Kentucky hills, we read the statement and committed ourselves to its implementation.

I think back to that powerful dedication ritual and reflect on the statement. It could be seen as a small, insignificant act with big words and promises. The big words and fervent commitment contrast starkly with the present devastating environmental reality and projections. What is now politically possible to address the crisis and what science affirms is needed are two very different things. The reality of the crisis is paralyzing, overwhelming. Alarm bells have been ringing with dire warnings, and as a society we are still hitting the snooze button, preferring sleep and our collective comfort to the cold jolt of awareness.

Courage is needed to face the reality of the environmental crisis without turning away or shutting down. Merton modeled this courage for us in the face of the reality of nuclear weapons, urging others to move beyond apathy or casual acceptance. "I do not think that

Catholics realize the situation at all. They seem to be totally unaware of the gravity of the hour spiritually speaking, quite apart from the physical danger. It may very well be that we are faced with a temptation to a total interior apostasy from Christ while perhaps maintaining an exterior rectitude of some sort. This is frightful."[1]

Merton's words are the context for the statement and for our monastic life in the United States. The Rule of Benedict, I believe, gives direction on where we might position ourselves now, in this situation. The Rule of Benedict places the porter at the door of the monastery close enough that anyone who knocks can be received with the warmth of love. Those who are poor, however, do not need to knock; they need only to cry out. The porter, listening at the door, is to respond.

In our day, it is not a stretch to include the cries of creation along with the cries of the poor. They are related. Humans who are poor suffer disproportionately from this crisis. Scarce resources, needed by all, are hoarded and wasted by the richest nations—including ours. The devastating effects of climate change already are felt in massive crop failures, droughts, tsunamis, hurricanes, mudslides, and fires. All of these are causing tremendous suffering, especially for those who are poor.

Jesus' special care for the marginal is echoed in Benedict's Rule and is part of the Catholic monastic legacy in the United States. It is often those who live in poverty who lead the way with transformational actions that are good for all of creation. For example, one of the most powerful and effective environmental contributions of Catholic U.S. monastic communities is that Wangari Muta Maathai, Nobel Peace Laureate from Kenya, was educated at Mount St. Scholastica College in Atchison, Kansas, and has stayed in relationship with the Benedictine sisters there. Her Green Belt Movement is credited with empowering women and planting over forty million trees. For this she was imprisoned, tortured, and persecuted, but persevered to become deputy environmental minister in a new reform government. She thanked the Atchison Sisters, "I can only try to live a life in which you can find your own values and ideals reflected because in many ways I am the other side of all of you." Wangari shows what abundant beauty one woman, motivated by love, can create.

It's not just the women. I had the privilege of visiting the Benedictine men in Haiti and found an oasis of green in the parched desert. Haiti, the poorest country in the Western hemisphere, is also the place where I have seen the most severe ecological tragedy—deforestation, mudslides, rivers dried up to contaminated trickles.

In that desert, up a steep hill overlooking the Caribbean, is Mons St. Benoit. There, fruit and vegetables grown on composted soil are shared with their poor neighbors. Trees are planted and replanted trying to keep pace with those chopped down by people desperate for a bit of firewood. Bee keeping, honey production, and candle making— all traditional Haitian crafts—are reintroduced in the area. Much of their energy comes from solar power in a nation as rich in sunlight as it is poor in other resources. The monastic presence in Haiti is an oasis and a refuge for humans and for creation in their part of the planet.

In addition to the models from the developing world, Catholic monastic communities in the United States are relating with new, creative, intentional communities and new forms of monastic life, some based on the Rule of Benedict, others looking to monasticism for models of living. Green Mountain Monastery, an ecozoic monastery based on the teaching of Thomas Berry, identifies itself as "in the dynamic tradition of Benedictine monasticism." Common elements of the rich variety of new communities that identify themselves as part of a "new monasticism" include moving to abandoned places and caring for the earth. They are intent on living more sustainably, and monasticism is their model.

I participate in an initiative identifying with the new monasticism and find much food for reflection in the experience. Three years after moving into a run-down abandoned house with a young couple, Jess and Matthew Ochalek, and naming it Mary the Apostle Catholic Worker, we're learning much, especially patience and long-term vision. We were enticed by Benedictine sisters Mary Lou Kownacki and Mary Miller to move onto the block and participate with others in transforming one of the worst areas of inner-city Erie to make it safe and beautiful, especially for the children. It was Merton who first identified the inner city as the new desert in need of monks. In her book *A Monk in the Inner City*, Mary Lou reflects on returning to this block, this abandoned place, to her childhood home to care for her aging father and then staying here because of the children.[2]

In our house, we started by filling dumpsters with trash, replacing doors and broken windows, fixing the porch, repairing the roof, adding heat the first winter, and putting in insulation the second. Siding is next on the list and the electrical rewiring is almost finished. Room by room, we patched, painted, carpeted. The downstairs bathroom—with compost toilet—and a second guest room are the last rooms and are almost finished. Jess and Matthew's baby, Brigid, was born six months after we moved in.

We could not have done all this without much help and donations from friends and supporters. The movement to live and renovate abandoned houses in urban centers instead of building new on green space is good for the earth on many levels, including reducing transportation for commuting, but it is also difficult to do. Renovations are time consuming and costly. But we found others with experience and interest in saving, restoring, and cutting waste while adding energy-saving options when we could.

Experiments with other eco-friendly ways of living are mixed as well. I travel by bike as much as possible. Some of our neighbors, though, have children and no cars and the lack of efficient, available mass transit is a real hardship.

Experimenting with no dryer or dishwasher, with gardening and rain-barrel water collection do save energy and resources but mean more time for daily tasks. I find some of them to be good mindfulness practices and ways to slow down. On the other hand, I am acutely aware that what we might experiment with, our neighbors do without choice. Some on the block have gone months without water or gas when they couldn't swing rent, food, medicine, and utilities. The harm of living in these conditions, especially in households with children, is overwhelming. The main learning for me in this initiative, really, has been a deeper awareness of what life is like for those on the margins of our society.

There have been improvements on this block, with most credit going to Srs. Mary and Mary Lou, who have poured their hearts into this one corner of the inner city. They have gathered friends, volunteers, and supporters. Four formerly abandoned houses now have families living in them and two more will soon. A nuisance bar has been demolished. One house, notorious for dog fighting, was demolished and is now a garden with space for a labyrinth. Neighborhood children in an Earth Force group work with us in the garden. Another formerly abandoned house is now a center that just hosted the first activities for children. Upstairs is an apartment where another Erie Benedictine, Mary Ellen Plumb, now lives. Flowering trees line the street. Last winter, the Earth Force kids offered their neighbors winterization/energy-saving help.

Is it chaotic? Yes, we are developing the practiced ear that distinguishes fireworks from gunfire—no shortage of either in this part of the city. We've had several break-ins, even money stolen from the baby's piggy bank. We can relate to the vulnerability felt by our neighbors, except that we always have the option and the resources to move out. On the other hand, we know most of our neighbors by name and we look out for one another. It feels more like a community than any neighborhood I've lived in.

Clearly, the overall impact is positive and even contagious. Whether it can really spread to other blighted areas of the city is an open question given the time, resources, energy, and commitment needed by many, many people. Beauty and hope, though, are both contagious. And bringing beauty and hope to abandoned places is essential to monasticism, whether traditional or newly born.

The prophetic core of monasticism reminds us to avoid the temptation of making a few personal lifestyle changes and thinking that's the answer. The magnitude of the environmental crisis, when faced honestly, exposes that as incomplete. Monastic wisdom through the ages also warns against the spiritually dangerous self-righteousness and the judgment of others that often accompany focusing on personal habits.

Monasticism warns about other spiritual traps at the heart of the environmental crisis: the greed, apathy, and sense of entitlement that allow us in the richest nation to use and abuse far more than our share of the earth's resources. Our society's greed and apathy, which we all share at some level, are the root of incredible suffering for others on the planet. The monastic gifts of gratitude, reverence for the sacred presence everywhere, mindfulness, and the Catholic sacramental orientation are sought by many who look to our communities.

The prophetic witness of monastic life includes witness and action for political, social, and structural change. Benedict's porter, listening and responding with love to the cries of the poor, is our model. So is Thomas Merton, whose response to the horror of nuclear weapons can be a guide for our response now to the environmental crisis of the planet—which includes the nuclear threat. He combined strong words and numerous letters, encouraging, rebuking, preaching, and reflecting on the situation with deep love for the sacredness of all creation. My hope is that his encouragement could be extended to all forms of monasticism today and our response to the devastation of creation: "Let us then recognize ourselves for who we are: dervishes mad with secret therapeutic love which cannot be bought or sold, and which the politician fears more than violent revolution, for violence changes nothing. But love changes everything. We are stronger than the bomb."[3]

May we know this of ourselves.

VII

Appendix

The Spirituality of
Interreligious Dialogue

Shaping a New Ecological Consciousness

Dr. Fabrice Blée

A part from a few authors who refer to ecology here and there when they compare the Christian faith to other religions, the theology emerging from the praxis of interreligious dialogue has not yet given much attention to this area of concern. For example, when Ewert Cousins speaks of the "second axial period," he encourages axial religions to join together in giving attention once again to the earth.[1] For his part, Raimon Panikkar proposes a Christophany that is the fruit of dialogue between religions and cultures as well as of a respectful relationship to the environment.[2] But on the whole Christians engaged in the "dialogue of religious experience" are just beginning to become aware of the urgency of the ecological crisis.[3] Monastic men and women who engage in dialogue are a good example. Monastic Interreligious Dialogue was created in 1978, but only now, thirty years later, have these monks, whose practice of dialogue is recognized as especially advanced and profound, dedicated a major conference to this topic.

This essay, originally entitled "La spiritualité chrétienne du dialogue, creuset d'une nouvelle conscience écologique," was published in the April 2008 issue of *La Chair et le Souffle*, an international journal of theology and spirituality founded in 2006 by the faculty of theology of the University of Neuchâtel in Switzerland. It was translated by William Skudlarek, OSB, and appears here with permission.

That said, we need to note that the link between dialogue and ecology is not new. Over the past ten years it has been the topic of research and scholarly conferences, especially in the Anglo-Saxon world and often within the framework of ecofeminist theology.[4] The emphasis here is on interreligious cooperation between partners who already have a shared vision of nature, who recognize the urgency of finding a concrete solution to the ecological crisis, and who therefore call for a reform of their respective theologies.[5] Their search for consensus means that they give less attention to the specificity and coherence of the religious systems represented in the dialogue.[6] The way they enter into dialogue is determined by their ecological consciousness, and this, in turn, becomes the criterion by which they judge the relevance of any theology that would attempt to address the problem.

My approach, however, is to begin with the praxis of dialogue, specifically dialogue rooted in the Christian tradition. I then will try to show how this tradition promotes a respect for nature.[7] My goal is not to find a practical solution for one problem or the other, but to describe a way of establishing a relationship with nature that can give support to informed action in the future. In order to do this, I will pay special attention to two points. First of all, I will identify those elements of a Christian spirituality of dialogue that favor the adoption of a new way of thinking about nature and entering into a faith-inspired relationship with it.[8] Second, I will reflect on the dialogic approach to nature that flows from this new way of thinking. I will then suggest some future directions and will conclude by reflecting on how interreligious dialogue can mobilize Christians to participate in the work of resolving the ecological crisis.

A Spirituality of Dialogue That Suggests a New Approach to Nature

A Christian spirituality of dialogue is born when dialogue becomes a spiritual act, that is, when a relationship with another religion is no longer regarded as a threat to one's faith but a privileged place for its authentic expression. Such a relationship goes beyond physical encounter or mere conversion; it is a welcoming of others in their very "otherness," and leads to an interior or "intrareligious" dialogue.[9] Dialogue of this kind requires an attitude shaped by the virtues proper to every form of spirituality: love, faith, humility, commitment, detachment, fidelity, pardon, and so on.

For Christians the "dialogue of religious experience" is the most challenging form of dialogue because it requires that they love their "enemies." In the past Christians have regarded those who believe differently—the heretics inside and the pagans outside the church—as among these enemies. This is not to say that total openness to the other is the only kind of relationship that qualifies as authentic dialogue, but—given how demanding it is—if it succeeds, its ground rules and methods will certainly prove helpful to every other kind of relationship that aims to move from communication to communion, including our relationship to nature. This can be seen by looking at three characteristics of interreligious dialogue: the practice of hospitality, respect for otherness, and the liberation of the body.

The Practice of Hospitality

Becoming aware of the ecological crisis is one thing; doing something about it is another. How do we move from knowledge to action? Even more, what do we want to accomplish by our action?

These same questions need to be asked in a pluralist setting. We are enthusiastic about the idea of respecting other religions in order to live together in peace, but we quickly become discouraged when we try to put theory into practice and come up against difficult issues. We organize major conferences to propose a shared vision of the world and shared ideals—a praiseworthy endeavor, indeed, but one that puts us into a relationship with otherness. What makes others "other" is often their overarching religious vision and their understanding of the role of religion in bringing about peace. How can we arrive at a shared understanding of our situation, and what is to be done about it if we give little or no attention to the specific cultural, psychological, historical, political, or economic claims made by our partner in dialogue? To what degree is it possible to resolve a conflict with someone we do not know? How can we speak about interdependence if we do not experience it?

Monks who engage in dialogue are absolutely convinced that passing from knowledge to action necessarily involves the practice of hospitality. You can read every book ever written on the necessity of extending hospitality; you can issue all sorts of pronouncements about the necessity of living together in peace. Nothing will accomplish as much as actually entering someone else's world and receiving that person into our own, regardless of what we think about the individual and his or her beliefs.

What makes dialogue spiritual is the fact that it is not about theories but about life. Above all, it is praxis. It should not be confused with the study of religions or with working out a theory of unity with its principles and its rules. There is no way to become reconciled with believers from other religious traditions—or with nature, for that matter—if we do not allow ourselves to be challenged by them, not only on the intellectual level, but on the level of our life and our faith.

A spirituality of dialogue reminds Christians of the necessity of entering, heart and soul, into a relationship with nature that goes beyond our preconceptions and that is undertaken even before we have worked out a vision of the world that restores nature to its rightful place vis-à-vis human beings. When we do this, the earth is seen not as a thing we can deal with as we please, but as an autonomous living entity with which a human being can communicate as an equal, because—according to the language of faith—the divine Spirit is active at the heart of all creation.

Respect for Otherness

An ecological consciousness that leads to change does not come about unless we come back to the earth, allowing ourselves to be affected by its inherent logic and entering into a dialogue in which human beings and nature learn to live together for their mutual benefit rather than in a relationship of domination based on the belief that the one exists simply to benefit the other.

However, this return to the earth is not always accompanied by a desire to allow ourselves to be questioned by nature. Some try to understand the rhythms of nature for no other reason than to satisfy their desire to consume. This is why I am somewhat critical of the otherwise useful work of William McDonough and Michael Braungart, who propose a "cradle-to-cradle" approach to sustainable development.[10] They present nature as a vessel we have to look after and live in with care if it is not to sink. But our lifestyle does not have to change. Their approach is still very anthropocentric. There is no place for a dialogue that invites us to "mutual impoverishment."[11]

How do we rediscover the way to enter into communion with nature? Interreligious hospitality calls us to respect otherness. What this means concretely is that we are not to reject out of hand what we find unacceptable in other believers, nor to grab onto what we find familiar. We allow ourselves to be touched by the faith and beliefs that constitute their way of life and their purpose. This can be done, in part, by observation. However, the only way we will really understand and appreciate another's faith and religious practices is by making them our own in some way. Respect for difference comes about through a heart-to-heart encounter, through a relationship that strives for authenticity rather than for peace at any price, a relationship that, paradoxically, allows for the possibility of conflict. Dialogue does not flee from conflict. Rather, it clears away confusion and misunderstanding and thus gives rise to the hope that communication will lead to communion.

Spiritual dialogue teaches Christians that communion with nature also depends on an acceptance of otherness rather than on an *a priori* idea of the other's true nature and role. Spiritual dialogue thus predisposes Christians to come to a deeper understanding of the true nature of their partners in dialogue. These partners are always individuals. No one ever meets Islam or Buddhism. We enter into relationship with men and women who profess a particular religious tradition and who are endorsed by a given community.

By the same token, we never encounter "nature"—an abstraction used to designate a reality that can never be grasped in its entirety— but rather the disparate elements that constitute it without ever exhausting its richness and complexity. We cannot say we respect nature if we unthinkingly cause harm to what we consider insignificant. Likewise, we cannot claim to love humanity if we neglect our neighbor. At the same time, it is also true to say that the elements that constitute nature show us just how different it is from "culture." Nature is that which is not humanly conceived.[12]

These conflicting views of nature are not easy to reconcile and are sometimes expressed by contrasting the desire to free ourselves from the laws of nature that stand in the way of human freedom and the common good (the Enlightenment philosophies of the West) with the desire to be in harmony with nature by surrendering our egoistic tendencies (the Buddhist and Hindu spiritualities of the East, traditional religions). In both cases, nature stands over against the human by virtue of its *raison d'être* and its ultimate destiny.

Interreligious dialogue is also spiritual when it invites us to love the enemy, the stranger, the one in whom we cannot immediately recognize ourselves and who is seen as a threat to everything we stand for.[13] The practice of dialogue prompts Christians to act the same way toward nature, and to do so all the more because of the difficulties involved. In fact, the encounter with otherness, whether in the form of another believer or of nature, shows us the degree to which we are strangers to ourselves, both in our capacity for wonder and in our illusion that we can control the universe.

Liberation of the Body

How do we rescue nature from human exploitation? Ecofeminist theology responds by making the connection between the emancipation of nature and the liberation of women from the patriarchal domination that is also found in religious settings.[14] Personally, I believe that the close link between nature and the body—the body that has so often been identified with the feminine—is of the greatest importance for the issue at hand. Nature projects itself into the body and determines what it will be, even at the risk of being opposed to reason.[15] It forces us to deal with what we have suppressed.

The difficulty of entering into a relationship with nature is that its otherness is not simply because of its strangeness, but also because in certain ways it is too much like us. The more we cut ourselves off from the body, the more we become distant from nature and from ourselves. Is it not precisely this that characterizes modern society? We are all aware of the cult of the body, but the body that is worshipped is an artificial body, one that is opposed to nature. Underlying our determination always to demand more of the body and to go beyond its limits is our dream of achieving a perfect equilibrium, a universal ethic, tranquility, even a kind of immortality where happiness consists in our capacity to keep our universe static and without surprises. We go so far as to create virtual worlds more real than the natural world. In these worlds we are totally in control and the individual becomes a virtual "I" who now has to conform to new standards. The chasm that separates us from nature is growing wider.

Becoming more at home with our bodies can actually help us renew our contact with nature. Again, the interreligious journey can be of help. Christian monks in dialogue with Buddhist and Hindu contemplative traditions often rediscover that the body has a part to play in the process of "divinization."[16] Union with the divine does not take place in spite of the body, but in its very depths, in a body that is totally accepted. Numerous Christian practitioners have given witness to the ways in which zazen or yoga have helped them come to a more incarnated spiritual life.[17] Pierre de Béthune sees here an occasion for the theology of the incarnation to be given the kind of anthropology it deserves.[18] A spirituality of dialogue invites Christians to reappropriate the corporal dimension of spirituality and predisposes them to be reconciled to at least two of nature's characteristics: its impermanence and the irrationality of its power. First, the body mirrors nature in its movement, change, cycles of birth and death, fragility, and interdependence. In it are imprinted the rhythms of nature. One of the first things I learned about Zen meditation when I was in Japan was the power of nature, in its many variations, to bring me to experience the "I"—above all the embodied "I" with its sensations, feelings, and ideas—as constant change.[19]

The powers that lie hidden in the body are often in disarray and are only freed when one recognizes and accepts their natural rhythms. Within human beings there is an irrational nature, a collection of forces—some of them terrible, others sublime—that reason strives to contain in order to prevent a loss of control. In the West, where human beings think of themselves as masters of their destiny, one can see why people have welcomed the disenchantment of the world. A return to nature does not happen without crossing over into the hazardous realm of the unconscious where everyone has to enter into combat with monsters who demand to be recognized for what they are and insist that we mount them and ride off to discover new horizons.[20]

The Promise of a Dialogic Approach to Nature

A spirituality of dialogue sets the stage for an encounter with the natural environment in its otherness and also opens the way for a dialogic approach to nature that is capable of rallying and organizing Christians to come to grips with the ecological crisis. I highlight two characteristics of this approach: otherness as opposed to divinity and responsibility as opposed to anthropocentrism.

Otherness versus Divinity

James Lovelock puts forth the thesis that the earth is like a goddess (Gaia) who takes care of creation.[21] However, divinizing the earth is not the way to rally Christians, much less political and economic elites. This approach carries with it the double risk of returning to the superstitions from which the West has been able to free itself and of creating a new dogmatism.[22] Decreeing that nature is divine sets up a priestly hierarchy that monitors all that we need to do. There is no escaping it! Human domination is replaced by a biocentrism that, in turn, gives rise to a new religious and intellectual elite.[23]

Nonetheless, we must return to an understanding of nature as sacred. We might do that by formulating statements and coming up with theories that would affect public opinion to some degree. But nothing can take the place of a life immersed in nature, totally dependent on the natural environment. Such is the case with aboriginal peoples whose religion is most deeply rooted in a relationship to nature. For them nature is sacred not because of some *a priori* theology, even one that says we must protect it, but because they live in such a close relationship with it. The sacred is not an abstract idea, but something experienced.

Only those who are hospitable to nature and allow themselves to be questioned and transformed by it have the right to say that it is sacred. Otherwise we engage in romanticism, seeing nature as something that is graceful and beautiful, but forgetting that it is also harsh and cruel. The sacred is both breathtaking and intriguing (*mysterium tremendum et fascinans*);[24] we can also speak of it as something to be feared. But this only makes sense if we speak out of experience. The sacred only exists to the degree that it has been sensed. Revering nature as if it were something divine will be of no use in dealing with today's challenges.

What will help is a dialogic stance, an act of hospitality grounded in the silence of the Spirit. The earth is a living entity, but that does not make it divine. It is possible to enter into dialogue with it, however, allowing it to reveal its holiness within the space created by dialogue. In spiritual dialogue the stranger is certainly received as Christ, but that does not mean that the stranger is the Christ. Those who are unfamiliar are received as Christ in the sacred space of relationship. The one who practices dialogue is awakened to the presence of the divine Spirit in the other by coming face-to-face with his or her otherness. What this means is that nature is divine only to the eyes of faith.

Responsibility versus Anthropocentrism

Between the romantic vision of a Mother Earth to be worshiped and the stark view of nature as a savage entity to be tamed, there is the biblical understanding of responsibility or stewardship. We need to ask if this understanding is pertinent to our discussion.

There are those who believe that the concept of stewardship is to be rejected because it is anthropocentric.[25] However, what is to be rejected is an understanding of nature that subjects it to human beings. Nature must be given its autonomy and divine legitimacy. Spiritual dialogue in an interreligious setting does not summon people to unite around any particular divinity or God. Rather it demands that everyone be responsible—in accordance with their own tradition—for entering more deeply into the divine mystery, which no one can claim to monopolize. They do so by their willingness to enter the "desert of otherness."[26]

The desert is the symbol of the relational space to which Christians are called by Satan (the adversary), as was Jesus, to make a choice that will be decisive for their life of faith. Will they choose to be self-sufficient, or will they opt to submit themselves to God? Will they choose worship without love, or being reconciled first with their enemies (Matt. 5:23–25)? The position that human beings take is crucial for the creation of mutual understanding and peace. Even though everyone may believe in God, each individual still has to choose—in God's name—whether to reject the other or enter into dialogue. The same holds true for an individual's relationship with nature. People cannot be brought together by offering them a univocal understanding of the earth as a goddess coupled with a way of living on earth that would deprive them of their supremacy. If human beings are the problem, they are also the solution.

The notion of responsibility is not obsolete, but our understanding of it needs to be revised. Responsibility does not require us to become masters of creation, placing it at the service of our well-being. To be responsible for others means seeing to it that they become all they are meant to be, helping them become free people and not servants. The only way nature can be subject to human beings is if humans subject themselves to the divine Spirit, who radiates love (Rom. 5:5) and guarantees freedom (2 Cor. 3:17). Otherwise submission is the reverse side of tyranny. What is needed is a conversion to a new way of thinking about others and their environment, a conversion of heart that begins with oneself.[27]

The principal challenge of a spirituality of dialogue is combining the reception of the other with the abandonment of self-interest. There is no question here of anthropocentrism, because true believers do not find their center in themselves. Their center is in the divine power that is present and active in all of creation, but not identified with it.[28] This being the case, locating the origin of human beings outside the earth is not an obstacle to ecological conscientiousness.[29] On the contrary, as soon as humans allow themselves to be led by the Spirit, the Spirit enables them to see nature as the reflection (Eckhart) or the expression (St. Francis of Assisi) of God.

Even more, the Spirit shows them how to divinize creation through the selfsame Spirit by directing it to its destiny. When human beings submit themselves to God, they receive the gift of establishing peace with everything that surrounds them. All of nature becomes submissive to them, as can be seen in the lives of those saints whose simple presence was enough to pacify the most savage beasts. These saints offer us a glimpse of paradise, where the human race lives in complete harmony with its environment (Ezek. 11:1–9).[30]

Conclusion: The Manifold Dynamics of Dialogue

The dialogic approach to nature I have briefly outlined here does not call into question other interreligious approaches. We need to take into account the complex nature of dialogue in our relationship to nature. The link between ecology and dialogue can take different forms depending on the kind of dialogue undertaken: of life, of action, of experts, or of religious experience. The Anglo-Saxon movement referred to above (R. R. Ruether, M. E. Tucker, J. Grim, L. White, H. Eaton, and others) is, on the whole, directed to a dialogue of action in order to redress injustice. The emphasis is on cooperation between believers of different religions for the purpose of finding a concrete solution to a specific problem. The cause determines both the dialogue and the way it is articulated theologically.

The dialogue with nature is unique and urgent. At the same time, it should not be singled out as the only viable interreligious activity, thereby minimizing the many and varied dynamics of dialogue. As we have seen, dialogue at the level of religious experience is founded on hospitality as an expression of faith. This form of dialogue is often neglected, but it guarantees that relationships will not be self-serving and that they will be rooted in the silence of the Spirit. The dialogue of experts ensures that each new experience will be connected with one's own religious tradition. Theological dialogue is extremely important, even if it does not give priority to ecological questions.

There are some who criticize a theology of religious pluralism precisely because it does not give enough attention to the natural environment. It goes without saying that there is an urgent need to do so, but we cannot skip over important steps. If we do, we run the risk of creating a parallel movement on the margins of our traditions and justifying that decision by saying that peoples' attitudes are not changing fast enough.[31] If we adopt positions that are outside religious traditions, can we really expect to be able to rally those traditions around a cause?

Providing a theological interpretation of the praxis of dialogue allows it to have an even greater impact on our behavior and the behavior of those who will follow us. Only in this way will it be possible to persevere in our hospitable response to nature. In the end, each individual enters into dialogue according to his or her own charism; no individual or group can claim to exhaust all the possibilities. If Christians are to come to a new understanding of nature and devote themselves to its cause, collaboration among the different contributors is crucial, as is an understanding of dialogue as an ecclesial activity.

One of the greatest challenges Christians will face is learning to live out their faith by being open to those who pray and believe differently than they do. If Christians are to change the way they regard nature, they need to be open to religious otherness. Otherwise it will be impossible to become a part of the burgeoning movement that Ewert Cousins relates to the vision of Teilhard de Chardin: "He sees individuals deepening their autonomy by uniting the centers. In such a union both unity and difference are maintained in absolute polarity and creative harmony."[32] In this way religions can draw on and share their respective stores of spiritual wisdom, releasing the energy needed to create a "cosmic solidarity" that will lead to a new global ecological conscience.[33]

Notes

Introduction

1. The North American commission of Monastic Interreligious Dialogue (MID) is part of the international *Dialogue Interreligieux Monastique*/Monastic Interreligious Dialogue (DIMMID). More information on both DIMMID and MID can be found on their Web sites: www.dimmid.org and www.monasticdialogue.org.

2. Donald Mitchell and James Wiseman, eds., *The Gethsemani Encounter: A Dialogue on the Spiritual Life by Buddhist and Christian Monastics* (New York: Continuum, 1999). Republished as *The Spiritual Life: A Dialogue of Buddhist and Christian Monastics* (New York: Lantern Books, 2010).

3. Donald Mitchell and James Wiseman, eds., *Transforming Suffering: Reflections on Finding Peace in Troubled Times* (New York: Image, 2003). Republished by Lantern Books, 2010, as *Finding Peace in Troubled Times*.

4. Thomas Merton, *Working Notebook #34* (1968), unpublished manuscript (Louisville, Ky.: The Thomas Merton Center, Bellarmine University, n.d.), 34.

5. Thomas Merton, *When the Trees Say Nothing: Writings on Nature*, ed. Kathleen Deignan (Notre Dame, Ind.: Sorin Books, 2003).

6. John de Graff et al., *Affluenza: The All-Consuming Epidemic* (San Francisco: Berrett-Koehler Publishers, 2002), 4.

7. "Mind is the forerunner" (the first verse of the Dhammapada); "In the beginning was the word" (the first verse of the Gospel of John).

Paradise Regained Re-lost—Fr. Ezekiel Lotz, OSB

1. William Shannon, *Something of a Rebel: Thomas Merton, His Life and Works: An Introduction* (Cincinnati: St. Anthony Messenger Press, 1997), 136.

2. Ibid., 171 n. 3.

3. Monsignor Shannon *has* taken note, however, of Merton's great concern with modern technology, a theme intricately related to the topic of ecology. In fact, in the revision of his *Thomas Merton's Dark Path: The Inner Experience of a Contemplative* (New York: Farrar, Straus, Giroux, 1981), Shannon has added a considerable

amount of information involving Merton's interest in the work of Jacques Ellul and in the so-called double-edged sword of technology. See *Thomas Merton's Paradise Journey: Writings on Contemplation* (Cincinnati: St. Anthony Messenger Press, 2000), especially p. 306 of the book's index.

4. For what follows, see Thomas Merton, *The Seven Storey Mountain* (New York: Harcourt, Brace, 1948), 55ff.

5. Ibid., 56–57.

6. Michael Mott, *The Seven Mountains of Thomas Merton* (Boston: Houghton Mifflin, 1984), 74.

7. Ibid., 75.

8. Merton, *Seven Storey Mountain*, 126–27.

9. Mott, *Seven Mountains*, 78ff.

10. Ibid., 78–79.

11. Ibid., 79. Mott is quoting from Merton, *Seven Storey Mountain*.

12. Ibid., 45.

13. Ibid, 79. Mott again is quoting from Merton, *Seven Storey Mountain*.

14. Ibid., 206.

15. Ibid., 205.

16. Shannon, *Rebel*, 28.

17. Mott, *Seven Mountains*, 205. This theme of monastic enclosures serving as paradisiacal gardens predates Hugh of St. Victor by almost a millennium and is found in early desert fathers' writings as well as in those of early Celtic monks and hermits. See Michael W. Higgins, *Heretic Blood: The Spiritual Geography of Thomas Merton* (Toronto: Stoddart, 1998), 251ff.; and Kathleen Deignan, "Introduction: 'The Forest Is My Bride'" in *When the Trees Say Nothing: Writings on Nature*, by Thomas Merton, ed. Kathleen Deignan (Notre Dame, Ind.: Sorin Books, 2003), 34.

18. Monica Weiss, "Dwelling in Eden: Thomas Merton's Return to Paradise," *Riscritture dell'Eden: il giardino nell'immaginazione letteraria dell'Occidente*, ed. Andrea Mariani (Venice: Mazzaanti Editori SRL, 2006), 3:228.

19. Ibid., quoting Thomas Merton, *Entering the Silence: Becoming a Monk and a Writer*, ed. Jonathan Montaldo, vol. 2, *The Journals of Thomas Merton* (San Francisco: HarperSanFrancisco, 1996), 216.

20. Mott, *Seven Mountains*, 206.

21. Ibid., 209.

22. Ibid., 208.

23. Ibid., 228, 245.

24. Ibid., 246.

25. Ibid., 246, 258.

26. See Thomas Merton, *Dancing in the Water of Life: Seeking Peace in the Hermitage*, ed. Robert E. Daggy, vol. 5, *The Journals of Thomas Merton* (San Francisco: HarperSanFrancisco, 1998), 128, 136–37, esp. 294–95.

27. Mott, *Seven Mountains*, 259.

28. Ibid.

29. Ibid.

30. Ibid., 260.

31. Thomas Merton, *Witness to Freedom: The Letters of Thomas Merton in Times of Crisis*, ed. William Shannon (San Diego: Harcourt Brace, 1995), 70–71, italics Merton's. Also note Merton's journal entry for December 11, 1962, in reference to wanting to obtain and read Carson's book: "Someone will say: you worry about birds: why not worry about people? I worry about both birds and people. We are in the world and are part of it and we are destroying everything because we are destroying ourselves, spiritually, morally and in every way. It is all part of the same sickness, and it all hangs together," *Turning Towards the World*, ed. Victor Kramer, vol. 4, *The Journals of Thomas Merton* (San Francisco: HarperSanFrancisco, 1997), 274f.

32. Merton, *Witness to Freedom*, 71.

33. Ibid.

34. Ibid.

35. Donald P. St. John, "Technological Culture and Contemplative Ecology in Thomas Merton's *Conjectures of a Guilty Bystander*," *Worldviews* 6, no. 2 (2002): 166.

36. See Dennis Patrick O'Hara, "'The whole world . . . has appeared as a transparent manifestation of the love of God': Portents of Merton as Eco-theologian," *The Merton Annual* 9 (1996): 109f.

37. Merton, *Witness to Freedom*, 71.

38. St. John, "Technological Culture," 173.

39. Ibid.

40. Merton, *Witness to Freedom*, 71.

41. Quoted in *What a Way to Go: Life at the End of Empire*, written and directed by Tim Bennett (VisionQuest Pictures, 2008).

42. Merton, *Witness to Freedom*, 71.

43. Thomas Merton, *Conjectures of a Guilty Bystander* (Garden City, N.Y.: Doubleday, 1966), 60–61.

44. Ibid., 60.

45. Ibid., 64.

46. Ibid., 222.

47. Ibid.

48. Ibid., 222f.

49. Thomas Merton, "The Wild Places," in *Thomas Merton: Preview of the Asian Journal*, ed. Walter Capps (New York: Crossroad, 1989), 95.

50. Ibid., 96–97.

51. Ibid., 97.

52. Ibid., 98–99.

53. Ibid., 99.

54. Ibid., 101.

55. Ibid., 105–6.

56. Ibid., 106.

57. Ibid.

58. Ibid.,107.

59. Thomas Merton, "Preface to the Japanese edition of *Seeds of Contemplation: Kanso no shushi* (1965)," in *Reflections of My Work*, ed. Robert E. Daggy (London: Fount, 1989), 100, 103.

60. St. John, "Technological Culture," 179; and Merton, *Conjectures*, 25.

61. Weiss, "Dwelling in Eden," 241.

62. Ibid., 242.

63. Ibid, 241; quoted.

64. Thomas Merton, "Wilderness and Paradise," in *The Monastic Journey*, ed. Patrick Hart (Mission, Kans.: Sheed, Andrews, and McMeel, 1977), 150. (Noted with different wording in Weiss, "Dwelling in Eden," 242.)

65. Thomas Merton, *The Asian Journal of Thomas Merton*, ed. Naomi Burton et al. (New York: New Directions, 1973), 307.

66. Thomas Merton, *Working Notebook #34* (1968), unpublished manuscript (Louisville, Ky.: The Thomas Merton Center, Bellarmine University, n.d.), 34.

67. Bruno Barnhart, *The Future of Wisdom: Toward a Rebirth of Sapiential Christianity* (New York: Continuum, 2007), 39.

The World as Created, Fallen, and Redeemed—
Fr. James Wiseman, OSB

1. See Perry Schmidt-Leukel, ed., *Buddhism, Christianity, and the Question of Creation: Karmic or Divine* (Burlington, Vt.: Ashgate, 2006).

2. Avery Dulles, *A Testimonial to Grace* (New York: Sheed and Ward, 1946), 34.

3. Ibid., 50–54, *passim*.

4. Ibid., 65.

5. Ted Peters, "On Creating the Cosmos," in *Physics, Philosophy, and Theology: A Common Quest for Understanding*, ed. Robert John Russell et al., 3rd ed. (Vatican City State: Vatican Observatory Foundation, 1997), 288.

6. Keith Ward, "God as a Principle of Cosmological Explanation," in *Quantum Cosmology and the Laws of Nature*, ed. Robert John Russell et al., 2nd ed. (Vatican City State: Vatican Observatory Foundation; Berkeley, Calif.: Center for Theology and the Natural Sciences, 1996), 248–49.

7. Ephrem, *The Hymns on Virginity and on the Symbols of the Lord* 20:16–17, in *Ephrem the Syrian: Hymns* (New York: Paulist, 1989), 349.

8. Francis of Assisi, *The Canticle of Brother Sun*, in *Light from Light: An Anthology of Christian Mysticism*, ed. Louis Dupré and James A. Wiseman, rev. ed. (New York: Paulist, 2001), 119.

9. *Julian of Norwich: Showings*, chap. 5 of the Long Text, trans. Edmund Colledge, O.S.A., and James Walsh, S.J. (New York: Paulist, 1978), 183.

10. James A. Wiseman, *Theology and Modern Science: Quest for Coherence* (New York: Continuum, 2002), 107–8.

11. *Julian of Norwich: Showings*, chap. 5 of the Long Text, 184.

12. Lynn White, Jr., "The Historical Roots of Our Ecologic Crisis," *Science* 155, March 10, 1967, 1203–7.

13. Ibid., 1205.

14. Pierre Teilhard de Chardin, "The Mass on the World," in *Hymn of the Universe*, trans. William Collins Sons & Co. (New York and Evanston: Harper & Row, 1965), 22.

15. Jürgen Moltmann, *God in Creation: A New Theology of Creation and the Spirit of God*, trans. Margaret Kohl (San Francisco: Harper & Row, 1985), 11.

16. Perry Schmidt-Leukel, "Bridging the Gulf," in *Buddhism, Christianity, and the Question of Creation*, 167.

17. Ibid., 154.

18. Ibid., 176.

The Monastic Rules of Theravada and Mahayana Buddhism— Rev. Heng Sure, PhD

1. Throughout this chapter, I use the term "monks" as gender nonspecific, to refer to both male and female monks.

2. See www.ted.com/index.php/talks/al_gore_s_new_thinking_on_the_climate_crisis.html (accessed February 5, 2009).

The Monastic Instinct to Revere, to Conserve, to Be Content with Little, and to Share—Rev. Eko Little

1. Ross King, *Brunelleschi's Dome: How a Renaissance Genius Reinvented Architecture* (New York: Penguin Books, 2000).

2. P. T. N. H. Jiyu-Kennett, *Zen Is Eternal Life*, 4th ed. (Mount Shasta: Shasta Abbey Press, 1999), 146.

3. Ibid., 147–48.

4. Ibid., 149.

5. Ibid.

6. Ibid., 150.

7. Ibid., 160.

8. Ibid.

9. Ibid., "Shushogi: What Is Truly Meant by Training and Enlightenment," 100.

Christian Monasticism and Simplicity of Life—
Fr. Charles Cummings, OCSO

1. In one passage, the word *simple* (*akeraioi*) means "innocent," in contrast with "shrewd," when Jesus says to his disciples: "Behold, I am sending you like sheep in the midst of wolves; so be shrewd as serpents and simple as doves" (Matt. 10:16). Another word (*haplous*) sometimes translated as "simple" has the more precise meaning of "healthy" or "pure": "The lamp of the body is the eye. If your eye is sound, your whole body will be filled with light" (Matt. 6:22).

2. See St. Bernard of Clairvaux, "Reject what is superfluous and you are saved!" (SC 58:10; SBOp 2.134).

3. See the teaching of the Buddha on renunciation of desire or craving.

4. Thomas Merton visited Pleasant Hill before its restoration and describes one visit in his journal, using the word *simplicity* to sum up his impressions: "The empty fields, the big trees—how I would love to explore those houses and listen to that silence. In spite of the general decay and despair there is joy there still and simplicity. Shakers fascinate me" (December 26, 1959, *A Search for Solitude: The Journals of Thomas Merton*, vol. 3, *1952–1960*, ed. Lawrence Cunningham (New York: Harper-SanFrancisco, 1996), 362.

5. Words: American Shaker song, eighteenth century; music: Simple Gifts; meter: Irr. with refrain; http://www.oremus.org/hymnal/t/t717.html.

6. Her real name was Mildred Norman. For twenty-eight years she walked back and forth across the United States, logging more than twenty-five thousand miles, preaching peace, owning only what she could carry with her. She vowed to "remain a wanderer until mankind has learned the way of peace, walking until given shelter and fasting until given food." See: http://www.peacepilgrim.com/pphome.htm (accessed June 6, 2009).

7. See Jon Mooallem, "The Afterlife of Cellphones," *New York Times*, January 13, 2008; see also Felicity Barringer, "A City Committed to Recycling Is Ready for More," *New York Times*, May 7, 2008.

8. St. Ambrose, Commentary on Gospel of Luke, cited by the Catholic Bishops Conference of England and Wales, "The Call of Creation: God's Invitation and the Human Response: The Natural Environment and Catholic Social Teaching," 2002.

9. Slogan attributed to Horace Dammers, 1921–2004, Episcopal Dean of Bristol, Britain, founder of the Life Style Movement, UK.

10. For further reading on simplicity of life: Annabel Shilson-Thomas, *Livesimply: A CAFOD Resource for Living Simply, Sustainably, in Solidarity* (Norwich, UK: Canterbury, 2008); Beth Daley, "Going Green for Lent: Many Use Period of Penance to Aid Environment," *Boston Globe*, March 3, 2008; Santa Rita Abbey, "Gift of Simplicity," 2008, Santa Rita Abbey Web site: http://santaritabbey.org/GIFT%20OF%20SIMPLICITY.htm (accessed June 6, 2009); "Holy See: Planet Is Everyone's Responsibility: Archbishop [Migliore] Notes Pontiff's Efforts on Behalf of Environment," *Zenit*, ZE08021407 - 2008-02-14 - Permalink: http://

www.zenit.org/article-21777?l=english (accessed June 6, 2009); Chrysogonus Waddell, "Simplicity and the Abbot de Rancé," *Cistercian Studies Quarterly* 22 (1987): 250–61; Edward Readicker-Henderson, "Letting Go of Stuff," *Spirituality & Health* (January–February 2008); Gwynne Dyer, "The Coming Food Catastrophe," *FFWD: Calgary's News & Entertainment Weekly* (April 3, 2008); Jonathan Walmsley, "Reducing Your Carbon Footprint," *Mid Ulster Mail*, July 30, 2007, http://www.midulstermail.co.uk/midulster-news-features/Reducing-your-Carbon-Footprint-.3071003.jp (accessed June 6, 2009); Kris Berggren, "Going Green: Sisters Are Renewing Community Life From the Ground Up," *National Catholic Reporter*, February 22, 2008; Laura Lloyd, "Religious Orders Bring Clout to War on Bottled Water," *National Catholic Reporter*, January 11, 2008; Martinus Cawley, "A Monastic Experience and Theology of Waste Material Recycling," *Cistercian Studies Quarterly* 20 (1985): 237–48; Thomas C. Fox, "A Durable Future: Bill McKibben," *National Catholic Reporter*, November 16, 2007; Thomas Merton, *The Spirit of Simplicity: Characteristic of the Cistercian Order* (Trappist, Ky.: Abbey of Our Lady of Gethsemani, 1948).

Complicity and Conversion—Fr. Hugh Feiss, OSB

1. I owe this threefold distinction to an article by Elizabeth Johnson. "Creative Giver of Life: An Ecological Theology of the Holy Spirit," by Elizabeth A. Johnson, CSJ. The Spirit in the New Millennium: Fourth Annual Holy Spirit Lecture and Colloquium, Duquesne University, May 28–29, 2008.

2. Leszek Kolakowski, *Why Is There Something Rather than Nothing?: 23 Questions from Great Philosophers* (New York: Basic Books, 2007), 175–77.

3. Margaret Avison, "Exposure," cited by D. S. Martin, review *Momentary Dark*, by Margaret Avison, *Image* 51 (Fall 2006): 120.

Good Practices of Buddhist Monastic Communities in North America—Ven. Thubten Semkye

1. Michael Pollan, "Why Bother?" *New York Times Magazine*, April 20, 2008, http://www.nytimes.com/2008/04/20/magazine/20wwln-lede-t.html?ref=world (accessed June 6, 2009).

2. Thubten Chödrön, *Path to Happiness* (Singapore: Abitabha Buddhist Centre, 1999). For free distribution.

The Monastic Challenge to Respond in Love— Sr. Anne McCarthy, OSB

1. Thomas Merton, *Cold War Letters* (Maryknoll, N.Y.: Orbis Books, 2006), 10–11.

2. Mary Lou Kownacki, *A Monk in the Inner City* (Maryknoll, N.Y.: Orbis Books, 2008).

3. Thomas Merton, *Raids on the Unspeakable* (New York: New Directions, 1966), 160.

Appendix: The Spirituality of Interreligious Dialogue: Shaping a New Ecological Consciousness—Dr. Fabrice Blée

1. Ewert Cousins, "A Spirituality for the New Axial Period," in *Exploring Christian Spirituality: An Ecumenical Reader*, ed. Kenneth J. Collins, 83–92 (Grand Rapids: Baker Books, 2000).

2. Raimon Panikkar, *Une christophanie pour notre temps*, Le souffle de l'esprit (Arles: Actes Sud, 2001).

3. The "dialogue of religious experience" is one of the four forms of dialogue identified by the Pontifical Council for Interreligious Dialogue. The other three are the dialogue of life, the dialogue of work, and the dialogue of theological exchange. See *The Attitude of the Church toward Followers of Other Religions* (1964) and *Dialogue and Proclamation: Reflection and Orientations on Interreligious Dialogue and the Proclamation of the Gospel of Jesus Christ* (1991).

4. See the Forum of Religion and Ecology: http://fore.research.yale.edu.

5. See Rosemary Radford Ruether, *Gaia and God: An Ecofeminist Theology of Earth Healing* (San Francisco: HarperCollins, 1992).

6. Heather Eaton puts it this way: "The central task is to align religious efforts, and the spectrum of cosmologies, symbols, rituals, values and ethical orientations, within the rhythms and limits of the natural world" ("This Sacred Earth at the Nexus of Religion, Ecology and Politics," *European Journal of Science and Theology* 3, no. 4 (December 2007): 23–38). See the report of Mary Evelyn Tucker and John Grim, "Religions of the World and Ecology: Discovering the Common Ground" *Earth Ethics* 10, no. 1 (Fall 1998).

7. I am in agreement with Ewert Cousins, who holds that our survival depends on a new global consciousness, one that imposes a double task: "To enter creatively into the dialogue of religions and to channel their energies into solving the common human problems that threaten our future on earth" (*Christ of the 21st Century* [New York: Continuum, 1998], 10).

8. Especially the experience of monastic interreligious dialogue, whose history and challenges I dealt with in *Le désert de l'altérité. Une expérience spirituelle du dialogue interreligieux* (Montréal/Paris: Médiaspaul, 2004).

9. The term "intrareligious dialogue" was coined by Panikkar and refers to a dialogue that involves not only meeting people of other religions and studying their beliefs and doctrines, but also creating a space within oneself where one can meet others as others, heart-to-heart. Dialogue becomes not just an intellectual pursuit, but an existential concern, a spiritual act that brings together within one person "two ways of being, seeing, and thinking." See Jacques Dupuis, *Jesus Christ at the Encounter of World Religions*, trans. Robert R. Barr (Maryknoll, N.Y.: Orbis Books, 1991), 321; see also Raimon Panikkar, *The Intrareligious Dialogue* (New York: Paulist Press, 1999).

10. William McDonough and Michael Braungart, *Cradle to Cradle: Remaking the Way We Make Things* (New York: North Point Press, 2002).

11. Pierre de Béthune, *By Faith and Hospitality: The Monastic Tradition as a Model for Interreligious Encounter*, trans. Dame Mary Groves, OSB (Leominster, Herefordshire: Gracewing, 2002), 70–71.

12. According to Marini-Bettolo, nature is "the natural environment: that is to say, that part of the environment that has been not modified by human beings" (See René Coste, *Dieu et l'écologie: Environnement, théologie, spiritualité* (Paris: Éditions de l'Atelier, 1994), 8.

13. See "L'amour du lointain," in *L'hospitalité sacrée entre les religions*, by Pierre de Béthune (Paris: Albin Michel, 2007).

14. See Rosemary R. Ruether, *New Woman/New Earth: Sexist Ideology and Human Liberation* (New York: Seabury Press, 2004), 204.

15. The Enlightenment philosophers of the eighteenth century are proponents of this point of view, especially Kant, for whom the thinking subject stands over against the feelings and the natural inclinations that are characteristic of the individual insofar as the individual has a body.

16. See René Coste, *Dieu et l'écologie*, 105; Raimon Panikkar, *Intrareligious Dialogue*, 18–19.

17. "Contemplation et dialogue interreligieux: Repères et perspectives puisés dans l'expérience des moines," *Bulletin Secretarius pro non-Christianis* 84, no. 3 (1993). See Bulletin #70 on the Monastic Interreligious Dialogue Web site (www. monasticdialogue.org) for a collection of reflections by monks on the experience of interreligious dialogue.

18. Pierre de Béthune, "L'amour du lointain," 70.

19. Fabrice Blée, "Le milieu de la pratique zen : Pour une spiritualité du dialogue," *Origins* 3–4 (2003): 23–34.

20. From a Christian point of view, these words echo those of Pierre Teilhard de Chardin, cited by René Coste: "Those who passionately love Jesus hidden in the powers that give increase to the Earth will be embraced by the Earth, like a mother embraces her child, and brought to gaze upon the face of God" (*Dieu et l'écologie*, 237).

21. James Lovelock, *Gaia: A New Look at Life on Earth* (New York: Oxford University Press, 1979).

22. René Coste speaks of a "*régression archaïque*" (*Dieu et l'écologie*, 55).

23. Biocentrism is defended by "*deep ecology*," most notably by Aldo Leopold. It should be noted that this kind of dislocation can lead to the idea that ecology and pacifism have nothing to do with one another. According to William Aikin, "massive human death would be a good thing. . . . For the sake of our milieu, ninety percent of the human species should be eliminated!" (cited in René Coste, *Dieu et l'écologie*, 32).

24. See Sumner B. Twiss and Walter H. Conser, *Experience of the Sacred: Readings in the Phenomenology of Religion* (Hanover, N.H.: Brown University Press, 1992), 78.

25. See Heather Eaton, "This Sacred Earth," 38. The scientific community is divided about anthropocentrism. For example, Alfons Auer defends it, while others (e.g., Lynn White and John B. Cobb) reject it.

26. One can apply to this expression René Coste's contention that "the new style of life to which we are called today demands asceticism" (*Dieu et l'écologie*, 264). See also Fabrice Blée, "L'ascèse du dialogue," in *Le désert de l'altérité*, 193.

27. See Charles Birch, "Appelés à remplir la terre," in *Briser les barrières : Nairobi 1975* (Paris: L'Harmattan, 1976).

28. In this regard René Coste speaks of theocentrism (*Dieu et l'écologie*, 65, 100).

29. In Heather Eaton, "This Sacred Earth," 49.

30. See Cousins, *Christ of the 21st Century*, 193. "Human persons are most in harmony with themselves and the universe when they harmonize themselves at the depth of their being with God."

31. Isn't there a danger of this kind of marginalization when L. White holds that we have to find another religion or rethink the old one in the light of a particular understanding of nature? See René Coste (*Dieu et l'écologie*, 43, 71), who believes just the contrary, that "creation itself . . . has to be rethought in the light of the Mystery of Jesus" (95). That would seem to be Panikkar's position when he speaks of Christophany.

32. Cousins, *Christ of the 21st Century*, 178.

33. Raimon Panikkar, *Intrareligious Dialogue*, 35.

About the Editors

Fr. William Skudlarek, OSB, is a monk of Saint John's Abbey and administrative assistant to the abbot. In addition to having taught theology and homiletics at Saint John's University, he served as a Maryknoll Associate in Brazil and was a member of Saint John's Abbey's priory in Japan. During his years in Japan he began to practice zazen with the Sanbyo Kyodan. After serving for five years as president and then executive director of the North American branch of Monastic Interreligious Dialogue, he was appointed General Secretary of Dialogue Interreligieux Monastique/Monastic Interreligious Dialogue in September 2007. He is the author of *Demythologizing Celibacy: Practical Wisdom from Christian and Buddhist Monasticism* (Liturgical Press, 2008).

Donald W. Mitchell is a professor of philosophy at Purdue University. He is the author of *Buddhism: Introducing the Buddhist Experience* (Oxford University Press, 2008). He is also the co-editor (with James Wiseman) of *The Gethsemani Encounter: A Dialogue on the Spiritual Life by Buddhist and Christian Monastics* (republished by Lantern Books as *The Spiritual Life: A Dialogue of Buddhist and Christian Monastics*) and *Transforming Suffering: Reflections on Finding Peace in Troubled Times* (republished by Lantern Books as *Finding Peace in Troubled Times: Buddhist and Christian Monastics on Transforming Suffering*).